The
POWER
TO ACT

TRANSFORMING LITERACY AND EDUCATION

CINTHIA COLETTI HAAN

The

POWER
TO ACT

TRANSFORMING LITERACY AND EDUCATION

Contributions by
Richard Long and Elenn Steinberg

ISBN: 1466218258

ISBN 13: 9781466218253

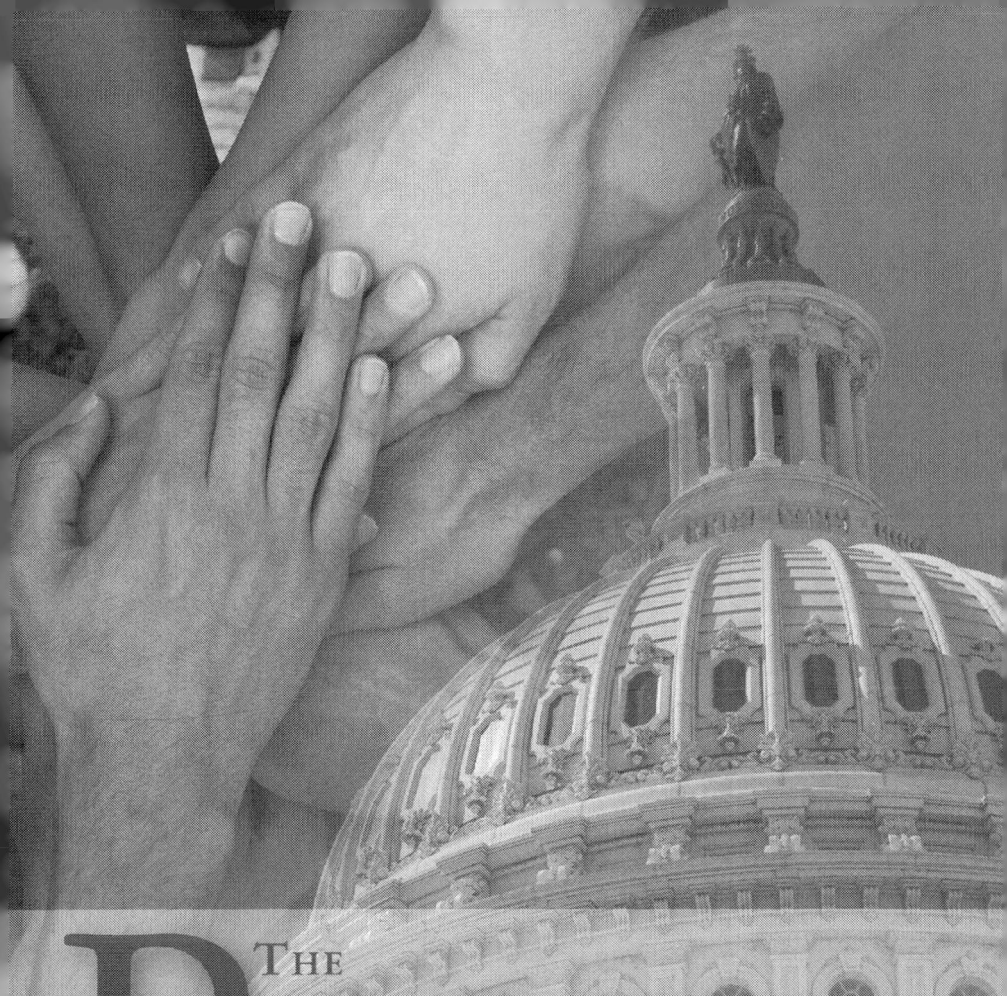

THE POWER TO ACT

TRANSFORMING LITERACY AND EDUCATION

CINTHIA COLETTI HAAN

CONTENTS

Chapter Three:

An Action Plan for Concerned Parents and

Chapter Four:

First Helping My Child, *Then* Creating

Chapter Five:

Chapter Six:

Chapter Seven:

Chapter Eight:

PREFACE

Seeds for Reading Literacy

The goal of this book is to unify all those who recognize the imperative for a literate and educated society into a single, persuasive call to action. Think of this book as a toolbox that provides the knowledge, the empirical data, and the materials for you to be an influential leader, capable of tackling the tough problem of literacy education in America today. Simply stated, learning is the trump card for human progress, and literacy is the root of lifelong learning. Sadly, as Americans we are failing to make literate tens of millions of our young citizens. This fact is threatening our country's future. In the text-driven culture of our twenty-first century, someone who is semi-illiterate has little chance of becoming a contributing member of society or finding gainful employment. And, employment is critical not only for individuals to support themselves financially, but also for the society to benefit from the talent of each member. America's greatest asset base is its human capital. Education, training, and health are a country's most important investments in its human capital. If America is to remain a world leader, the global economy demands that its citizens be prepared to participate in and compete with an international workforce that is rapidly becoming more skilled. America must invest in the skills of its young people, and literacy is the bedrock for a world-class education.

As reported by the National Assessment of Educational Progress (NAEP), also known as the Nation's Report Card[1], America is not investing wisely in education. Shockingly, only three out of ten fourth- and eighth-grade students read at a proficient level; the other seven have just basic or below-basic reading

---

1 National Assessment of Educational Progress, The Nation's Report Card (Washington, DC, 2009).

skills. How can that be when this nation spends more than half a trillion dollars each year on public school education? Further, an alarming 47 percent of our urban students drop out of high school[2]. Facts like these are frightening. But even more startling is America's literacy ranking among international communities[3]. Overall, the Organisation for Economic Co-operation and Development (OECD) ranks U.S. students in the middle of the pack: fourteenth place in reading literacy among thirty-four developed nations. Can you believe countries such as Poland, Estonia, and South Korea[4] do a better job teaching their students to read than the United States? Science has determined that all but a very small percentage of students can become reading literate: able to read for knowledge, write accurately and coherently, and think critically about printed material so they are able to analyze, critique, synthesize, and use information to reflect, make informed decisions, and create new ideas. If empirical data confirm that we know how to teach reading literacy, then why don't we?

You may ask yourself why I use the term "reading literacy." My experience in education has given me the opportunity to interact with a number of philosophical camps on reading—deans in colleges of education, superintendents of school districts, principals, classroom teachers, neuroscientists, reading researchers, and professional education therapists. Over time, these camps have debated reading theory, seldom bridging their divide. I believe that while no single camp is 100 percent correct, together they offer a symphony of triumph. Without question, the pressures on both

---

2 America's Promise Alliance, Johns Hopkins University, Everyone Graduates Center, Civic Enterprises, Alliance for Excellent Education, "Building a Grad Nation: Progress and Challenge in Ending the High School Dropout Epidemic" (Washington, DC, 2010).

3 Programme for International Student Assessment (PISA), Organisation for Economic Co-operation and Development (OECD), Paris, France (2009).

4 Organisation for Economic Co-operation and Development, Programme for International Student Assessment (PISA) Ranking, OECD Community, Paris, France (2009).

reading and literacy have changed over time with society's advancements. Therefore, "reading literacy" is a consensus-building term that expands beyond reading's required development of active and interactive skill attainment and beyond comprehension of rich text. In today's fast moving world, the demands for reading literacy include employing strategy and skill as well as cognitive function, all of which are necessary for lifelong learning. Reading literacy implies that there is a capacity for reflection on written material that initiates personal experiences and memories. Reading literacy moves from the school room to the work place, to citizenship, to lifetime learning, which fulfills or is central to achieving an individual's aspirations. As our world evolves, we must give our citizens the tools to fully participate—to fulfill dreams, achieve goals, and enrich their lives.

Learning to read is a complex process,[5] and teachers of reading need to be knowledgeable, highly skilled, and capable of teaching diverse student populations. Many people believe pre-kindergarten to third-grade (PK–3) teachers should be professionals as educated and valued as engineers, medical doctors, and attorneys. The only way to accomplish this is for the U.S. to fundamentally transform education leadership in the way teachers are recruited, trained, assessed, and compensated. This represents social justice for both our students and our teachers. To this end, I believe, an all-encompassing state literacy law is essential because science has confirmed that upon entering the third grade, students must be prepared to commence the journey of text comprehension so that by the fourth grade and beyond they are reading literate, able to think about classroom materials and formulate their own ideas. Guaranteeing literacy skills for all students is the only way to ensure that America has a capable citizenry—young people receiving an effective, motivating, and challenging education.

---

5 Maryanne Wolf, Proust and the Squid: The Story and Science of the Reading Brain, (New York, NY: HarperCollins, 2007), 130.

You may be asking, why state law and not federal law? In recent decades, the federal government funded many worthy programs that rewarded states for improving reading rates. Many of these programs had significant impact and brought about relevant cultural change. However, with each new administration come new ideas with consequent changes in funding that hinder deep-rooted sustainability. After reflecting long and hard upon this national reality, many experts have concluded that only state legislation, created through community leadership, can achieve vital literacy acquisition for all students. State literacy law(s) can create the actions, learning tools, implementation, and systemic sustainability required to educate *all* young people, irrespective of their neighborhood. High educational standards must be inclusive.

We know there are a variety of reasonable and unreasonable reasons why so many of our young people have not been taught reading literacy. It often comes down to the pretext of human populations, which is nonsense. For the past decade, I have had the honor of visiting some of the highest performing—yet most demographically challenged—schools in our country. They are often called "90/90/90" schools: 90 percent or more of students are impoverished and eligible for free and reduced lunch, 90 percent or more belong to ethnic minority groups, and 90 percent or more meet or exceed state standards in reading and English language arts. After personally observing these students working with their teachers and principals and actively engaged in learning because they have mastered reading literacy skills, I have *zero* concern about the aptitudes of *all* American students, regardless of their school's diversity, home environment, classroom size, and all the other excuses. What haunts me is that so many in our nation seem indifferent to the potential of these youth. Thus, from this point forward, I refer to these students, often typecast as uneducable, as our SEEDS students, and I ask you to do the same. Seeds, because they all have the potential to bloom, grow, and contribute to society.

The acronym of SEEDS evolved slowly. The concept of identifying students who aren't reading as a result of poor instruction and the lack of classroom support systems came to me as I sat in a school district meeting last year. By mid-morning I was infuriated as I listened to teachers and administrators classify fourth- and fifth-graders as "challenged" because they were failing their classes. Well, obviously they were failing! Every student was two or more years behind grade-level reading ability and justifiably "challenged" because he or she was unable to read his or her grade-level books, write papers coherently, or pass written exams. It was heartbreaking to hear these educators speak about these students as if it were the children's fault they were failing. I wanted to shout, "It isn't their fault! The blame belongs to our system for failing to teach them reading in grades PK–3! The blame belongs to the colleges of education for failing to prepare and train our teachers on the complexities of reading development." If our education system, including professional development for existing teachers, had paid attention and done their jobs, these students would be reading literate, gaining knowledge and passing their science, history, social studies, math, and every other class! After that meeting, I reached out to a group of colleagues and we created the SEEDS acronym for students who are not taught to read. SEEDS are Struggling readers, Economically disadvantaged youth, English language learners, students with Dyslexia and Specific learning disability students. Many SEEDS struggle because they are the recipients of inappropriate instruction in the early grades; others struggle because of the nature of their environments; some because of biological reasons; and a growing number because they are just starting to learn English. Regardless of the reasons, we possess the research and tools to ensure that all but a few percent of students can attain reading literacy. Like seeds in all of nature, they have the potential to grow into valuable, capable citizens.

What is not acceptable is to remain complacent, especially when we read the tea leaves about America's future. We should not tolerate the sense of resignation that public education today produces unqualified, uneducated young citizens. We must have the will and conviction to turn this ship around, to be the optimists that harness American will, talent, and energy to drive the changes needed for a literate, educated nation. If not, our country will fall into both social and economic anguish. We will experience a continuation of record high unemployment. We will see an increase in the $14 trillion national debt, which is closing in on our gross domestic product (GDP). Society will be increasingly burdened by welfare services. We will witness GDP erosion as global market competition is exacerbated by the offshoring of multinational manufacturers hiring "highly skilled" foreign workers. There will be scarcer opportunities for low-skilled jobs as a result of the continuing evolution of information technology, insourcing, technical automation, workforce software, and virtual staff. We will be unable to "refill" domestic jobs after the exodus of retiring, skilled, highly educated baby boomers (coined the "baby-boom echo"). In addition, functional illiteracy leads to an increase in prison populations. Now, both you and I would like to ignore these facts because we believe America is a superpower country of great ideals and achievement. And that was true in the last century—America was filled with promise and incredible innovations. But we live in a very different global society today, and we cannot afford to ignore that reality. As American citizens, every one of us must rise to the challenge.

It is implicit that an educated populace possesses the productivity that will affect its ability to employ, compete, and get richer over time. Science has shown that we can abolish functional illiteracy in our young people and prepare them to become gainfully employed citizens and lifelong learners. In a day and age when superior, differentiated teaching models and professional development modules give us the instruments to ensure all students are reading literate, it is a moral imperative that we direct these tools into the hands of educators—from preschool to university—to reverse the current illiteracy, functional illiteracy, and semi-literacy trends in our great nation.

We have no more time to waste. We allowed a slow decline in literacy standards and, as a result, American young people are unable to pick up the reins. My colleagues and I want to help empower all stakeholders in a mission to create state literacy law and build grassroots support systems in every state. We have taken more than a year to study and evaluate science, best practices, and existing laws within a number of states. Each law we examined provided different components to achieve student reading proficiency; however, none of the laws was complete on its own. We have prepared for you an exceptional description of model legislation, based on decades of empirical data. The work will guide you and your legislators to the principles necessary for reading literacy achievement so all students can become lifelong learners ready for the global, twenty-first-century workforce. This book will provide you with proven strategies for building grassroots teams and working with state government officials. In such ventures, it is often difficult to know where to begin. To help you, this "toolbox" was created by using focus groups, attending conferences, reaching out to experts, and interviewing "superstars"—those that have successfully enacted or made great strides toward sanctioning new legislation. As you embark on this path to help secure America's future, we will support you. Together we will spur our society back to strength through its young and, most importantly, we will preserve the capacity of American students to seize hold of their own lives and flourish like nature's seeds.

With hopes and appreciation for all you do,

Cinthia Coletti Haan

Co-Founder and Chair, The Haan Foundation for Children

President, Power4Kids Reading Initiative

Vice President, Board of Directors, International Dyslexia Association, and

Chair, Government Affairs Committee

Chair, Literate Nation

www.state-literacy-law.org

CHAPTER ONE
PLANTING SEEDS: CREATING A CALL TO ACTION

---

*"Human history becomes more and more a race
between education and catastrophe."*

—H. G. Wells

We find ourselves living in notable times of reevaluation and change. Many believe that voter trust in national government is eroding, and perhaps the role of state governments is strengthened and preferential for solving state issues. State governments allow us to establish action plans built on areas of agreement. Today, in state after state, we find ourselves agreeing on the topic of public education—it isn't working. Education data have confirmed that problems of American student literacy are weighty, critical, and require drastic action. In a recent OECD6 literacy study of thirty-four nations, America's fifteen-year-olds finished fifteenth in reading literacy scores. Where America once led the world in college graduation rates, it now ranks fourteenth among the top twenty-two developed countries. Worse, within these countries, America has the eighth lowest high school graduation rate. These statistics represent a chilling certainty: "educational gaps impose on the United States the economic equivalent of a permanent national recession."[7]

Sadly, almost all education statistics paint bleak realities for the future. At the same time, this gives states a great opportunity to enact powerful change. History has shown us that Americans excel at creating grassroots groups to solve society's most difficult problems. Stories in history, from the Declaration of Independence to civil rights, veteran rights, women's rights, working conditions, and environmental initiatives, confirm America's amazing ability to form organizations that create great change. Today, America has an enormously complex problem—educating its young citizens—that if not solved will spread weakness throughout society. Clearly, there are many hurdles that students face, from poverty to absentee parents, from untrained teachers to learning disabilities. But they are not excuses for the continuing increase in the rate of failure to teach children to read. The ramifications of illiteracy are disturbing for every one of us. According to the McKinsey report *Economic Impact of the Achievement Gap in America*, failing to educate our youth generates lower individual earnings, poor health, higher rates of incarceration, and significant forfeiture of America's GDP. The time has come for us to quickly and powerfully build community organizations to solve the fundamental, singular problem

---

6 Organisation for Economic Co-operation and Development (OECD), Paris, France (2009).

7 "The Economic Impact of the Achievement Gap in America's Schools," McKinsey & Company (2009) San Francisco, CA, http://www.mckinsey.com/app_media/images/page_images/offices/socialsector/pdf/achievement_gap_report.pdf, 17

that is key to the U.S. educating its young people. The education system is plagued by myriad problems, from lack of leadership, professional development and teacher preparedness, to crumbling schools, old technology, top-heavy officialdoms, budget deficits, tenure issues, reduced school days and shorter school years, poor reading skills—and the list goes on. But let's look at the last two issues for a moment.

When we ponder why OECD assessments have American students doing the deep dive in international standings, both reading literacy and the number of hours a student is educated stand out. Compared to many OECD countries, American students have the shortest school day, spending a mere thirty-two hours a week in school. Countries such as Denmark and Sweden boast staggering forty- to fifty-hour school weeks, almost 30 percent more than America. The discrepancy with China is even starker. Among all countries, China's Shanghai and Hong Kong have seized two out of the top five rankings in the OECD International Reading Literacy standings. You may also know that China is rapidly becoming the number one English-speaking country in the world. What you may not know is that China's students spend between eight and a half hours to twelve hours a day in school.[8] This means China's children are spending roughly 50 percent more time being educated than America's children. Furthermore, China's teachers are chosen from the top ranks in their secondary schools, afforded an advanced college education and stipends, and appointed a mentor upon graduating—a seasoned master instructor to train under until he or she is deemed an "expert" teacher in his or her subject. China is intelligently making education its top priority with the knowledge that this is crucial for the country's success. While the U.S. conceives the basics of solid student reading literacy and correlated education hours, the fact remains that in state after state,

---

[8] "China's Children Too Busy for Playtime," *China Daily* (Xinhau), accessed September 15, 2011, http://www.chinadaily.com.cn/china/2007-05/13/content_871182.htm.

budget cuts require cutbacks to professional development and to the number of school days in each year. America must reprioritize the education of its young people and this commences with resolving the pinnacle problem that trumps all others: student reading literacy. Later in this book, we will touch upon a significant, unifying effort that created the Common Core State Standards Initiative ("Standards")—standards designed to be inclusive of all students and to transform schools to produce students capable of lifelong, twenty-first century learning. As of today, forty-five states have joined the initiative with the goal that all students, regardless of where they live or what school they attend, will meet the same, high-quality standards and all students will graduate high school prepared for college or the workforce. While I fully support these Standards, I fear they may never be realized for one key reason: the void of grade-level reading proficiency. Many experts believe the Standards will fail unless we support each student to achieve literacy proficiency, which requires that teachers (whether PK–12 teachers, reading specialists, or content areas teachers) receive intense professional development in order to become highly skilled professionals at promoting reading literacy. It is then the Standards can be achieved and reading literacy will move from the schoolroom to the work place, to citizenship, and to lifelong learning, which is central to achieving an individual's aspirations. And, only then, will American education stand a chance to get back on track as a world leader.

As Colin Powell noted on *Meet the Press*,[9] "America is going to be a minority nation in one more generation. Our minorities are not getting educated well enough now. Fifty percent of our minority kids are not finishing high school. We've got to invest in education." Not finishing high school should not be an option for any student in the twenty-first century. I cannot even begin to grasp the psychological costs of dropping out of school, much less the fact that there is no viable future for these young people impaired

---

9 NBC News, Meet the Press, New York, NY, April 17, 2011, Television.

by functional illiteracy, which is the primary reason for not finishing secondary school. A life without the ability to read a ballot in a voting booth, to clearly understand directions on prescription medications, to help a child with his or her homework, or to complete a job application is no life at all. Our forefathers wrote of the unalienable rights to life, liberty, and the pursuit of happiness, yet in some school districts, sixty percent of high school students would not be able to read those words. Colin Powell is adamant that fixing our nation's education system is paramount to America's future and reading literacy is the first crucial step because it leads to literacy in math, science, computers, and ultimately "industry literacy" that is necessary to succeed in one's job.

A friend of mine who does cognitive neuroscience research on the reading brain recently gave a lecture in Berkeley, California. She told me something rather unusual that captured one of the primary reasons I began this book. In her lecture, she had been describing her concern that children's immersion in digital media might impede the formation of an "expert reading brain" and might give children less motivation for coming to their own thoughts, insights, and creative ideas. While speaking, she noticed a small man dressed in the black uniform of the wait staff, pacing back and forth behind the audience. He seemed riveted by what she was saying and took notes. After the lecture, he waited until everyone left and then came up to her. He seized her hand and spoke more animatedly than anyone in the audience about his appreciation for what she had been saying. And, he told his story. Ali is a well-educated Iranian, who was forced to flee Iran decades before. He loves this country that allowed him to form a new life for himself and his family; but now he despairs for it. With an eloquence that was at once compelling and discomforting, he said, "America is losing its ascendancy," that its children couldn't read, do math or science, and that his chosen country will soon lose its place in history because we have let this happen. "Our children become 'dumber' every day," Ali said, while other nations do everything they can to make their children succeed.

When my friend, Maryanne Wolf, author of the highly ac-claimed book *Proust and the Squid: The Story and Science of the Reading Brain*, related Ali's heartfelt indictment of American society, we were both a little quiet as we sat outside by the sea. Whether our own interests are propelled by a desire to preserve society or to preserve the potential of each child, Ali was right. For a host of reasons, a great many of our American children are becoming only a fraction of what they could become, with implications for the whole of society that reach into the immediate, near term, and dis-tant future. Depending on what we do, we will all be either twice blessed—with thriving citizens in a thriving society—or twice cursed. The choice is ours.

The wonderful thing about reading literacy and a student's edu-cation is that almost everyone understands the two are intrinsically linked. Reading literacy provides the basis for all other accomplish-ments in education, job and career, hobbies, knowledge attainment, self-esteem, social status—ultimately, the quality of life.

As many of you know, College Board, the organization that ad-ministers the SAT test, began in 1900 with the goal of creating the first examination to expand access for students to attend college. Then and now, the examination helps admissions departments de-termine whether or not a student is "college-ready." College Board has data on student scores dating back to 1972. With great dismay and a ton of feeble excuses, College Board announced that the 2011 SAT student scores were the "lowest in 40-years."[10] Yes, you read this correctly. Even worse is when you study the report and learn that of the 1,650,000 students who took the exam, only 43 percent met the "college and career benchmark." Now, let's think about this for a moment: 1,650,000 "good" high school students took the SAT in 2011. These are the students who are passing their courses, taking

10 *"43 Percent of 2011 College-Bound Seniors Met SAT College and Career Readiness Benchmark,"* College Board, accessed September 17, 2011, http://press.collegeboard.org/releases/2011/43-percent-2011-college-bound-seniors-met-sat-college-and-career-readiness-benchmark.

AP classes, and earning a diploma. These are not the 1,230,000[11] students who drop out of secondary school each year, or the 1,000,000-plus students who are not qualified to graduate high school at all, yet still receive a diploma. No, these are the "good" students, which means that if only 43 percent are "college-ready" then roughly six out of every ten "good" students are *not* college-ready. This means that almost one million students (940,500) of the 1.65 million who were proud to take the SAT, each believing that he or she was a "good" student, ready to commence the journey into the world of higher education, will find out that he or she may be enrolled in *remedial* English classes. The fact that SAT scores for college-bound seniors have hit a forty-year low is miserable for our society, but more depressing is the poor education and preparation provided to our youths—it is catastrophic. Public schools are society's key resource for teaching its citizens to become productive, to have a basis from which to make informed decisions, and to participate in society.

The SAT and high school dropout statistic makes me think back to what Ali said to Dr. Wolf, "Dumb people are easily manipulated." And history highlights this truth. Thus, when education fails to prepare our youths for the future, the base of our society fails, which is essentially what Ali, the solid citizen, the employed manager of a respected establishment, was saying. The goal of this chapter is simple: We need everyone we can reach to fully comprehend the collective problems of the U.S. literacy and education breakdown. Our job is to "emotionally move" everyone we can to employ the solutions we already possess—solutions that will sustain our freedoms and our quality of life through an educated populace.

---

11 Editorial Projects in Education, Diplomas Count 2008, "School to College: Can State P–16 Councils Ease the Transition?," special issue, Education Week 26, no. 40 (2008).

We Must Stop the Noise

Before we can move forward, we must confront the unfortunate reality that much of literacy education has devolved into a polarizing debate over whether people are "for" or "against" scientifically based reading instruction for students and preparation for teachers. Often, the voices in the middle are crowded out by extreme positions on both sides. We must come together and stop the blame game, stop the noise, and solve the problem with a common voice: All kids will be reading literate and all teachers will have the skills to teach to a variety of diverse students. Working with a number of experts on both sides of the debate, we agree on a term of reading literacy for the twenty-first century.

As I mentioned, "Reading Literacy" is a term that has evolved over time with changes in society, the economy, and cultures. According to the Organisation for Economic Co-operation and Development, reading literacy transfers from childhood, to employment, to social responsibility, to lifelong learning, which is central to achieving an individual's dreams. Reading literacy also affords the reader interaction with peers and communities and continuing through interactions with large bureaucracies and complex legal systems. To attain reading literacy, a student must be taught to first utilize a wide range of reading and literacy skills that will develop into subject matter literacy—the building block to seek, to use, and to understand all theme material. Reading literacy unleashes the potential to enrich the breadth of experiences in an individual's personal life.

This term unites both sides of the reading aisle. Together we can end these dividing debates about literacy failure in our students and cultivate an atmosphere in which we can understand the major issue: Reading development culminates in literacy attainment. When you take a minute to think about it, the truth about learning to read is simple: Human beings are not born to read. Reading is an invention, and this means two important things. Genetically we do not possess "a reading circuit" in our brains like we have "a voice circuit," for example. We have to learn to read, be taught to read. The difference is that some children learn to read by exposure to almost any method; some children need very direct methods of being taught; and all teachers of reading need to be taught what works best for different children. Teachers can't teach what they have not been taught. It is simple and possible to advance preparation programs, professional development, and certification requirements for teachers of reading. In so doing, they will become our most respected, best skilled, highest paid, and keenly desired teachers who will carry the key responsibility of setting the foundation for all student academic achievement.

I had the honor, through the Haan Foundation, to co-lead an extraordinary clinical research project that incorporated neuroscience with reading research in public schools. Using science-based reading instruction programs, quality professional development, and functional magnetic resonance imaging (fMRI), we observed students' brains actually change how they function with the acquisition of reading skills. There were hundreds of students in the study from both the third and fifth grade. After just one hundred hours of small group instruction these children, who were reading at the bottom of their class, most likely dodged the bullet of becoming a high school dropout statistic. Extensive research demonstrates that all but a few students can be taught to read with known methods. Falling anywhere short is unconscionable. I predict that in three years, the implementation of the Common Core State Standards Initiative[12] will have both citizens and legislators aghast. Once this happens, intense focus will be directed to pre-kindergarten through third-grade reading and English language arts standards, along with requirements for each content area teacher in grades four through twelve to provide academic language instruction in

---

12 National Governors Association, Council of Chief State School Officers, "*Common Core Standards Initiative*," (Washington DC), 2010. http://www. corestandards.org/

their coursework. Let's hope that at this point if not sooner, state legislators will stand ready to help you pass literacy law.

We know students are emotionally, genetically, and environmentally different. It really doesn't matter. We can reverse this cycle of literacy failure by having the courage and conviction to stand up and say, "enough is enough," and demand dramatic improvement in the way we teach reading and prepare our teachers. We must unite as leaders—parents, grandparents, teachers, principals, communities, and politicians—all of us.

First Steps—Understand, Move, Pledge

> *"We must be the change we
> wish to see in the world."*
>
> —Mahatma Gandhi

Now that we can move beyond the controversies, we must pledge ourselves to engage in settings and venues that enable literacy law. Law that propels one goal—all students literate, capable of receiving an education and contributing to society. The words *"all* students literate" may seem like an obvious mantra; but we have yet to internalize it as a united voice in our quest for education. Ignore it, and nothing else matters.

You will note that I keep repeating the word *all* as well as key phrases. This is for transparent reasons. As with you, I too am tired of the debates and the division. Only the end goal matters—*all* students literate is the moral imperative and the human right that unites us. Second, I will repeat key messages so they may become your sound bites to be used in your own settings. They have been tested with focus groups and found to be the most potent in raising public awareness and generating support for educational causes. The more potent our work, the easier our journey.

Our tasks for student literacy are neither too complex nor too difficult. They are accomplished in three stages: (1) writing model literacy law based on what we know works; (2) initiating and forming a call to action that organizes through social networking in your schools, churches, communities, businesses, and state; and (3) designing a clear tactical plan that outlines the steps necessary to enact literacy laws, find legislative champion(s), and manage the political process. Stage one is accomplished. The model law has been written and is available to you online (www.state-literacy-law.org). This book is designed to become your toolbox of knowledge and materials needed to draw large numbers of people from every corner of society to push literacy legislation. In each step, don't forget the power of social media and networking. As an example, Lady Gaga tweets have rallied millions of young people to drive change on human rights (such as Don't Ask, Don't Tell), politics in foreign countries, clean energy, and you name it. A perfect example of the power of social media motivating change in multinational corporations is Gap. When Gap attempted to unveil a new logo guess what happened? "Gap has announced on its Facebook page that it is scrapping its new logo design efforts, acquiescing to a torrent of criticism coming primarily from Facebook and Twitter users."[13] How impressive is the power of social media? Very. Together we can quickly commence a wave of change using social networking, especially if we involve our children, adolescents, and teens to work together with us in a unified voice. They, too, want to be educated, good students, and they know that the system is failing their generation. Ask them to join you in the networking—our young people can be the muscle to

---

13 Ben Par, "Gap Reverts to Original Logo After Social Media Backlash," *Mashable Social Media*, October 11, 2011. http://mashable.com/2010/10/11/gap-logo/

move our message beyond all dreams. Collectively, they can stand up for their rights and mandate that they be taught to read and graduate high school ready for college and career. They can say in a vast voice of strength, "It is not our fault! Change it!"

In this chapter I will describe the critical ways to communicate facts and emotion to assure success in grassroots and networking campaigns. The next two chapters will outline the tactical steps and critical elements needed to build successful advocacy: (1) the idea—fixing something that is wrong; (2) the organization—assembling your team of networking advocates; (3) the champion—the legislator(s) who will take up the issue as his/her/their own; and (4) the process—managing efforts. The final chapters will tell success stories, address tips for parents advocating for their children, provide sample communiqués and scripts to a call-to-action campaign, and a summary of the model literacy law. And in the last chapter, I will share my personal, profound reflections that drive me today.

Your Call to Action Will Help Future Generations

We all agree it is our civic responsibility to give our children and grandchildren the skills, knowledge, and preparation for life. Every student should be literate. Every student should graduate from high school prepared for life—for a postsecondary degree or skilled in a profession. No exceptions. This is an American right; this is social justice; this is a moral imperative.

> *"...unalienable Rights, that among these are Life, Liberty and the pursuit of Happiness."*
> —United States Declaration of Independence, 1776

In all we do and say, it is important to remember who we are as a nation of people. Our focus groups have highlighted that as a people, Americans want this country to be "exceptional" in every aspect. The word "exceptional" is not well represented by the current political climate. How we consider ourselves politically doesn't matter. Whether we are extreme liberals, radical conservatives, or somewhere in the middle, the context of world history shows that the principles of liberty protected by our founders in our Declaration of Independence, and later in the U.S. Constitution, led to an inconceivable level of prosperity, safety, and happiness in this country. To this end, our collective will and action inspire our states' politicians to embrace the principle of "opportunity" in literacy, education, transformations of schools, and teacher preparation. American principles of liberty that led to self-reliance, equity, and social justice in our young country will help enact literacy laws so that all students have the opportunity to be exceptional.

Be mindful that good communication does not attack or accuse. It provides hope, a solution, and the plan, backed up by facts. Three goals must be accomplished in any successful call to action. First, we must be effective in showing positive, results-driven outcomes. For us, the outcome is for all students to become literate, able to learn academic subject matter, and earn an education (American equity). Second, we must motivate our friends, teachers, communities, social networks, and like-minded organizations to personally become committed to our literacy goal: making certain students are educated to become gainfully employed and contribute to society (American self-reliance). Third, we must challenge our education communities to be student-centered, encouraging the pursuit of excellence for each student (American social justice). We are everyday people who can unite across race and class to lead our states to literacy laws that take action *against* the status quo and regain the American dream through quality public education.

I am optimistic. We are a country of opportunity with plenty of experience and a great track record of doing big things, hard things together. America is passionate about wanting a world-class education system for its young, so don't hesitate to play the America card. Ali's strongly worded concerns for America's loss of its former "ascendancy" represent the feelings of many people whose energies and passions we can channel into positive change. What is wonderful in today's age of instant communication is that in short order we can get millions of followers to drive positive, vital change, simply by tweeting and posting on Facebook.

Compelling Communication

There are many things to remember when communicating your call to action, but none more important than knowing you have one message and one goal—all students literate. From your earliest stages of gathering your teams of like-minded supporters to working directly with politicians and their staffs, your call to action should constantly highlight your singular goal in a clear message about who and what the goal will affect. Messaging needs to be crafted carefully. A good way to test messages is through focus groups. Focus groups are as old as time and currently fashioned as a marketing research tool, adapted for inquiry in many fields, such as medicine and the social sciences. The knowledge acquired is often invaluable to a goal, such as politicians crafting messages for their constituents' vote and corporations seeking to expand market share into new demographics. You can conduct informal focus groups within your own communities.

For education messaging, The Word Doctors, a powerhouse firm in the profession of message creation, found that education communications have the most impact when they do three things:

1. Elicit feelings.

Your message needs to elicit a personal feeling or Americans won't get involved. It needs to be about you and them—my kids, your kids, his kids, her kids, the kids who play in your neighborhood,

America's kids. People respond best to a humanized message that is not about numbers and statistics, but about kids. (Give a sense of the personal.)

2. Emphasize equality.

Your messages need to be about equality, motivating everyone to join in your efforts. Literacy and a good education are rights for every student, every family, every hometown, and every community. Your messages are not just about rich kids or kids with dyslexia or English learners or inner-city kids; they are about every kid. (Equality is inclusive.)

3. Use images.

Your messages need to communicate through imagery, both positive and negative. Prompt in your audience their own imagination about the education of their children, their grandchildren, the next generations, and their country. Share your stories and ask about their stories. (Be creative.)

Communicating a sense of the personal and conveying equality are less tricky than evoking imagery. Here we need to be mindful of what images invoke and whether they enlist agreement or rejection. Focus groups have shown that a powerful, positive education image is seeing teenagers wearing caps and gowns, graduating from high school, ready for life's next step, coupled with equality words such as "Every student. No exception." This image allows the audience to agree with the theme and invokes in their imagination the students going off to college or into the workforce, or a combination of the two. Effective images elicit agreement with your message. Another positive image features younger kids shown in school, happy and engaged in learning. Your goal is to establish, quickly, agreement with the messages you are conveying.

Negative imagery must clearly denote what happens when we fail our children. In so doing, keep in mind that images of students failing are compelling and that failure images should never include teachers. These images divide our cause, because it is our belief that if our teachers are provided data-validated, quality preparation, and professional development, they will have the skills to ensure academic success. Just as it is not a child's fault that he or she cannot read, it is not the teacher's fault that he or she was not prepared to teach the complexities of reading development to a diverse group of students.

As with positive images of agreement, you can do the same with negative images. Potent negative imagery is a test sheet with a large, red "F" circled in the top, left-hand side of the page. This elicited the highest positive "agreement response" from the focus groups. They agreed that a grade of F was not acceptable and that something needed to be done to change it. Further, the group had empathy for the student rather than disgust. The next most powerful image was of a fourth-grade girl sitting at her desk sadly, holding her head up with her right hand, staring at her schoolbook with a downhearted facial expression. It elicited the response that she needed help; she wanted to do her work but couldn't and was very sad about it. The third best response was to an image of a forlorn sixth-grade boy standing in front of a green board holding a paper with an "F" in red that had been angrily written on the top of the page. The focus group felt that he had studied and tried his hardest, yet was unsuccessful. They felt that he needed help, that his failure wasn't his fault and that he could succeed with proper support. These images all led to agreement within the focus groups that the message was correct: The current educational system is failing our kids—our kids are not failing the system. Visit www.state-literacy-law.org to download these images.

Many exceptional documentaries also convey agreement about using negative images. I believe the title of Patrick Ireland's upcoming documentary, *Can't Read, Go to Jail*, says it all. Another strong image is the illiterate young man in prison, clearly unprepared for life, working hard to learn to read and achieve his GED. What else was there for this youth other than crime? He couldn't read text, resulting in his inability to learn in any of his school subjects; for this reason he could not graduate from high school, and once that happened he could not read well enough to fill out a job application, follow directions, or write a coherent paragraph about himself. What is wrong with this picture? These youths are our kids—America's future—and for too long we have allowed them to be shuffled through a broken system. We want them to achieve the things they dream of, yet we don't give them the tool they most need to accomplish these dreams. No wonder they are sullen and angry. Wouldn't you be? In most cases, the messaging can be this simple. In your call to action, use imagery that is clearly understandable: Kids have not failed us; their schools have failed them—we have failed them.

Your call to action will need to reach your local and state newspapers, television stations, and every and all social networks. Powerful communication will raise understanding of the reading problem and help everyone understand your planned solution: state literacy law. Additionally, working with local organizations will attract new members to your grassroots campaign, making you more powerful in arenas where you may not have yet engaged. Emails and letters to the editor remain one of the most important resources communities have to draw attention to their cause. We have added sample emails and letters for your perusal in Chapter Six. Another successful tool is to get individuals in your community to sign a document requesting literacy law (this can be done electronically). You can also get signatures from both small and large businesses in the community, a united voice demanding a better workforce through quality education that begins with reading literacy. This will go a long way toward encouraging a legislator(s) to support your initiative.

And, finally, while effectively communicating a sense of the personal, equality, and imagery, don't forget to communicate not just from your email and website, but by using the extraordinary potential of others' social media/networking groups. Get everyone to communicate the messages as their messages—blog, tweet, and use Facebook, LinkedIn listservs, and email with gusto. There are more than four hundred social media and social networking sites. Use all the beautiful social networking roads given to us in this century, for they are an amazingly expedient landscape from which to build support for your call to action, keep your teams informed, and inspire your legislators to accomplish your goal—all students literate. Within short order, you could have a million folks involved. While communicating, remember your language should be visual, descriptive, and imaginative. Micro and macro blog, tweet, ask America to join your cause. In no time, you will have thousands of followers.

> *"I'm a great believer that any tool that enhances communication has profound effects in terms of how people can learn from each other and how they can achieve the kind of freedoms that they're interested in."*
>
> —Bill Gates

Don't "Wing It"

Plan your call to action carefully. The goal is to move people from the problem to the solution by explaining why the literacy law is critically important: because it will solve America's huge societal issue of its students being unable to read, achieve the Standards, and perform in a global economy. Design your campaign thoughtfully and strategically. As Rich Long describes in the next chapter, be clear on your idea of what needs to be done and why.

In our case, our idea commands institutions to make all students reading literate: According to NAEP, almost seven in ten fourth- and eighth-grade students read *below* proficient, which means *only* three in ten students are being taught to read proficiently! If this were an exam, we would fail—30 percent is a grade of "F." Explain that these figures can be more than "nine and a half in ten students" reading proficiently *if* each kindergarten through third-grade classroom had certified teachers of reading, skilled and capable of teaching reading to a diverse student population. Explain that reading literacy will solve the leading problems of high school dropout rates and high prison populations. Explain how our communities and our country require an educated populace to flourish in this global economy. And, explain that it could mean the difference between a student going to college or going to jail, between America staying on top or America losing its ascendency.

Your success will depend on your preparation. Practice your message, learn your facts, ensure your mission is clear, follow your tactical plan, and enable and encourage your advocacy group to do the same. Get fired up!

> *"Success depends upon previous preparation, and without such preparation there is sure to be failure."*
>
> —Confucius

Advocacy Empowers

Across the world, there is no more singular unifying influence than education—both communities and a society are either fueled by it or volatile without it. Just take a look at the poor neighborhoods in your city. The volatility is apparent in the homes, on the streets, and in the schools. Hope is bleak. More than half of the young men and women will have dropped out of high school, angry, as they should be, having been given no tools, even the basics of literacy, to change their course. Think of the countries around the globe with the lowest literacy rates—Somalia, Afghanistan, Haiti, Nigeria, Rwanda, Pakistan, to name a few[14]—it takes only a moment to understand the unrest of these citizens with no optimism, no skill, and no opportunity. This isn't rocket science. Your literacy call to action will empower folks to get involved so the American dream continues. No one wants to see his or her neighborhoods or country become volatile because folks lack the basic skills to be self-sustaining. Advocates are in every corner and you will find them. Once a person understands that literacy, as the platform for education, is the foundation for all of life's success, the call to action is hard to ignore. Within this context, strangers quickly become allies.

When I am at social events, conversations frequently touch upon what I am doing. I flow easily into my concern and passion for a literate nation. Most people are perplexed at first. I like to get the conversion going by dropping little "knowledge-bombs," as I call them. For example: "Did you know that most people living below the poverty line are functionally illiterate? Yes, sadly, we now have more than 46 million Americans living in poverty[15], which is the highest it has been in *52 years*! Does this concern you as much as it does me?" Little knowledge-bombs like these always fuel conversation that leads to discussion on the need for a world-class, highly skilled, and educated workforce. Next, moving on to compare the astronomical high school dropout rates in the United States to South Korea's college graduation rates is guaranteed to get folks fired up and out of their seats (if they were in them)!

Strive to build and empower an army of invested individuals and groups that will get folks fired up—emailing, tweeting, blogging, and, whenever possible, visiting congressional leaders. As with most

---

14 "Countries With the Lowest Literacy Rates," *UNESCO (United Nations Educational, Scientific, and Cultural Organization)*, accessed August 2, 2011, http://www.sil.org/lingualinks/literacy/prepareforaliteracyprogram/ countrieswiththelowestratesofl.htm

15 Sabrina Tavernise, "Soaring Poverty Casts Spotlight on "Lost Decade." *The New York Times* (Washington) September 13, 2011.

things involving the government and bureaucracies, many people simply don't know what to do. They are not pleased with the status quo yet they are not quite resigned to failure, either. For too long they have heard people talk about the challenges of public education, an immense bureaucracy too large to fix. And, now they can do something about it because you have the first tangible step to a complex solution. You have given them a logical and binding goal that will empower them because it has a commonsense, understandable remedy: Literacy law requiring that all children and young people are taught to be reading literate. It is smart, it is clean, and it will have straightforward, deliverable, and accountable results.

Be Confident—Commit and Engage

I don't say this lightly: You can be confident that few issues have the potential to transform *every* aspect of American life as much as literacy and education. You can have confidence in building a team capable of taking the reins because the facts, tools, and messages are assembled.

> *"Never doubt that a small group of thoughtful, committed citizens can change the world; indeed, it's the only thing that ever has."*
>
> —Margaret Mead

Together you will need to commit on many levels. Commit to learn grim truths about the lack of student grade-level reading in schools, about pitiful high school graduation rates, about the dismal consequences functional illiteracy has on communities, the workforce, and the GDP in this text-driven world. Learn about the reality of the military's inability to find qualified young men and women to serve because joining requires graduation from high school. Learn about the cost for your community to support those who are not educated enough to support themselves.

I have found, however, that it is inevitable there will be divergence of opinion among those who are engaged in this work. Use this as an opportunity rather than a problem. Personally engage and encourage everyone to build relationships of trust with both those who share views and those holding divergent positions in literacy policy. Insist that our shared goal of landmark law must trump and bridge differences for the sake of all young people and for the sake of all teachers. Build trust for the goal by allowing room to listen and learn from one another. We need everyone behind the new ethos—all students learning to read, all teachers achieving professionalism in their trade.

To quote a good friend of mine, Dr. Jim Lanich, who is passionately devoted to education and leads the Educational Results Partnership, "We know how to teach reading, but we don't. Do you want to know why? Because we don't have to!" Jim is a bright and passionate former teacher who now "lives" education on the world stage. Jim calls it the way he sees it. He pulls no punches, and he personally aches for the kids he knows can be a success but who are doomed because of the U.S. education system. This book is all about taking Jim's statement, "Because we don't have to!" and turning it around to say, "Let's *have* to!"

Put Pressure on Politicians

Recently I attended a conference to hear Dr. Frank Luntz, author of *The New York Times* best-seller, *Words That Work: It's Not What*

You Say, It's What People Hear. Luntz best summed up political will-power: "We all know that deep down politicians don't act, don't move, don't actually do anything unless we put pressure on them. We have seen a lot of significant changes when people organize and force politicians to act." As a result of my own experiences, I am 100 percent in agreement with this sentiment and know that to enact the literacy law we desire, we must commit ourselves and persuade others to join us.

To our politicians, we dutifully make the statement that we are "unwilling" to accept the status quo of student literacy failure in our schools today. The message to our politicians is a reiteration of this chapter, "We demand more for America's future—all students can become productive citizens, but without reading literacy they have little choice but to turn to crime and social services. We demand action now for them and for us."

Whether working with one legislative champion or a group of champions in your state, you can create a ripple effect that will give inordinate momentum to get the bill through legislation and into law. This begins when you start calling for meetings and get moving with your champion(s). Use the "personal, equality, and imagery" ideas with your legislation. Here is a good introduction for politicians: "Surely the benefits of living among educated people resonates with you." This invokes images of solid citizens and good neighbors—every politician's desire for his or her constituents. "Surely you understand the consequences of living among the uneducated in society." This imagery of consequences influences people, physically and emotionally. "Surely you understand that crime, prison populations, high school dropout rates, and people's need for social services is, more often than not, the direct or indirect result of functional illiteracy." Not one politician in office can refute this (well, maybe one). Share with him or her the solution and ask him or her to support your goal. Whenever possible tie the work into achieving the Standards.

> *"I like to see a man proud of the place in which he lives. I like to see a man live so that his place will be proud of him."*
>
> —Abraham Lincoln

Remember, American politicians are influenced by the concept of the American dream. They, too, want to depend on good schools to educate their students to become respectable citizens and fine community supporters. Why? Because it leads to good property values, good jobs, good GSP (gross state product), and their reelection. However, they should not be reelected when more than 30 percent of public school students can't graduate from their high schools. With confidence, share with your state representatives that their constituents want school accountability, responsibility, and change, and that the first step is to enact literacy requirements to change the paradigm. Remember the words: Student literacy is a social right, a human right, and a moral imperative, without which students will fail, teachers will fail, schools will fail, and the burden on these individuals on society will become unbearable. Not addressing this issue is immoral.

Overcome the "Costs" Barrier – A Budget Mandate

Just like citizens who lived in the shadow of the Great Depression, we find ourselves facing the challenges of boosting student learning and graduation rates with decreasing funds and a rising national deficit. It is no mystery that with budget cuts, high unemployment, and recession-driven sales and income tax levels down, states are hard-pressed to meet their education obligations. The somber truth is that states are unlikely to accomplish any learning goals, even the praiseworthy new Standards, as I said before, until they solve the literacy failure rates in schools. With this realization comes the fact that hundreds of thousands of high school students earn a diploma only to realize their education fell short and, if they are accepted into college, remediation in reading and writing will be required before they can begin their credentialed subjects.

Let's take, for example, our most populated state, California, with more than 37 million people. How many high school graduates in California do you think are college-ready? How many will wind up in remedial classes repeating work they should have already mastered if they reach college? Well, the numbers and the price tag are probably far more than you ever imagined—the price tag blows my socks off. The Pacific Research Institute (2011) released a landmark study showing that failure to prepare a single cohort of freshmen for college-level work will cost them, their colleges, and the state up to $14 billion annually. Yes, $14 billion! How can this be? The study found that the majority of students going to two-year and four-year colleges will need to take remediation classes and, pathetically, the real remediation problem started long before the students entered college—it most likely began in early-elementary school. On average, only one in four high school students achieve grade-level proficiency or higher in English language arts on the California Standards Test; worse, barely one in five high school juniors are deemed college-ready in English language arts, according to the state's Early Assessment Program. This is heartbreaking, really. How sad is it for a young person to learn that after graduating from high school, getting good grades, and taking Advanced Placement classes, that a college semester or two of remedial classes in English language arts or math is needed? I can't even imagine the personal disappointment, much less the cost to the state of $14 billion a year. Just think, each year $14 billion could be directed for quality professional development, rebuilding crumbling school buildings, extending the school day, or providing quality after school programs to needy kids. Instead, these funds go to college remediation, which is tantamount to malpractice.

So regarding the cost barrier, I say there isn't one! The barrier is inertia; change is needed, now. And it begins with the universities and colleges of education that are ill preparing teaching candidates. It begins with new qualifications, professional development, and certification to be a skilled, teacher of reading (before he or she is allowed to teach children in the classroom). If we just make these two changes alone, the public benefits, in the long run, will far exceed any and all costs associated with re-tooling our teachers. Costs are quickly recaptured when all students are reading with understanding, writing their thoughts coherently, expressing themselves by using proper grammar and appropriate vocabulary, engaging in analysis, critiquing ideas, and making informed decisions as literate, participating citizens. Isn't this what education and ultimately college are all about— actively thinking and communicating thoughts, ideas, and opinions so one can contribute individually to his or her community—rather than attending remedial classes so he or she will understand college-level text?

Let's think of it this way. If only one in five high school juniors is reading proficiently, how in the world will the other four be able to achieve a postsecondary degree, which many experts believe is a bare minimum for gainful employment today? Will the other four even earn a high school diploma? Statistics tell us that only one in three students entering grade nine each year can expect to graduate in four years with the skills needed to succeed in college and the workplace. So what happens to the other two students? Unfortunately, this is what happens to them. Every year 1,230,000[16] students fail to graduate from secondary school, ac-

---

16 Alliance for Excellent Education—The High Cost of High School Dropouts: What the Nation Pays for Inadequate High Schools (Washington, DC: Author, 2008).

cording to a report by the Editorial Projects in Education Research Center. These 1,230,000 non-graduates cost our nation more than $319 billion in lost wages, taxes, and productivity over their lifetimes[17]. And, that is just one tragic year of wasting America's paramount asset—its human capital. We talk about the "cost barrier" to transform literacy education, but I prefer we think about it as the "revenue opportunity." Saving just one year of 1,230,000 students from failing to graduate high school will more than pay for all the literacy law requirements for decades and then some. We can even take this "revenue opportunity" a step further. If over the thirteen years these students are in elementary, middle, and secondary school, the same number graduated high school, the U.S. would realize from them more than $4 trillion in wages, taxes, and productivity. Isn't that enough said? Literacy law is a revenue generator.

Regardless of the fiscal crisis, the presumed cost barriers and the assumed revenue opportunity, the system must "right itself" and invest in human capital, its future. It must *first* address student literacy attainment and certification for teachers of reading *before* any money is spent on conventional education. This is not a budget issue; it is a budget *mandate*. It is not about how much we spend, but what we spend it on. In the reality of this recession, we cannot afford to make a single mistake in education funding allocations. All resource decisions need to be smart and strategic. Smart money must be about student-based money; smart money must be about data to track student reading acquisition and learning; smart money must be about strict system accountability that signals student learning matters most; smart money must be about retooling our teachers of reading; smart money must be about graduating our young citizens; smart money must be about investing in America's future through education. Bottom line: Take smaller budgets and make smart-money decisions focused on the heart of education.

---

17 Demography as Destiny: How America Can Build a Better Future (Washington, DC: Author, 2006).

Reading literacy equals diplomas, jobs, greater tax base, reduction of the national debt, and a more fulfilled society. If we don't act now, it may be too late.

For the first time in our nation's history, this generation is not as literate as the previous generations; worse, the baby boomer generation is getting ready to retire, leaving a skilled, educated workforce vacuum. These facts could be the most important issues facing our nation in the past forty to fifty years. To maintain our superior democracy, we cannot have inferior education. This strongly affirms that literacy law is a budget mandate. Otherwise, how are we going to compete with the world? America the superpower once led the world in college education; now we are twelfth in the world and sinking rapidly. For me, a literate nation is the societal imperative of our time. We need ethical and prudent leadership. We need to make student achievement-based, smart-money decisions in our education budgets. We need to rally, demanding political leaders reverse the decline of U.S. education. We need to invest expertise and science into retooling our teachers. And don't think for one minute that this problem can be fixed by simply throwing more money at it and expecting to see different results. We spend plenty of money already.

According to OECD, among the top twenty-five industrialized nations, no country spends more public and private money to educate each student than U.S. taxpayers. America spends more than half a trillion dollars each year on an education system that statistically fails a significant percentage of its youngest citizens. So, no, we are *not* getting value for our tax dollars spent; we are not making smart-money education decisions. And yes, if we do not command change through legislation, we stand to lose our freedom and millions of American stand to lose the opportunity to reach their dreams. As Bill Maxwell of the *St. Petersburg Times* so eloquently put it, "Literacy is especially important in this country because we are a democracy. Here, unlike in non-democratic nations, government wants and expects citizens to make good individual decisions. To do so, we must be literate and be able to comprehend the issues that are important to the greatest number of people over time."[18] With a continuing shift of societal power to a functionally illiterate populace, we will collapse the land of the free.

The Power to Act

Together we are poised and determined not to remain silent and inactive as this crisis looms. We must become the leaders of change. There should be no doubt in any person's mind that literacy development is an ongoing process that requires a sustained investment beginning in kindergarten and continuing through elementary and secondary school. You can personally contribute. You don't need money; you need commitment and time. You must call for social networking, community involvement, and political action on a grand scale. There is little more meaningful than ensuring all young people in your state are prepared for a contributing role in society—whether ready for college or career—and ultimately ready for the challenges and opportunities of life in a global economy.

Imagine an America that once again has the best and the brightest children, taught by the best teachers, in an environment of real learning. Everyone benefits—families, neighborhoods, communities, the economy, your state, our nation, our world. In the end, of course, it is not about who is the best, but about how to bring the best out of our children, the seeds of our shared future. Thus, we must invest ourselves in education. We must plant the seeds for our shared future so citizens can participate in freedom and attain their dreams, whatever they may be: career, culture, innovation, arts, sports, literature, technology, adventure, hobbies, charity, and all that our world offers. I know we can do this!

---

18 Bill Maxwell. "Literacy is Freedom." Accessed August 17, 2011, Rolemodels. jou.ufl.edu/rolemodels/publisher/literacy.shtm.

"Citizenship comes first today in our crowded world. No man can enjoy the privileges of education and thereafter with a clear conscience break his contract with society. To respect that contract is to be mature, to strengthen it is to be a good citizen, to do more than your share under it is noble."

—Isaiah Bowman

CHAPTER TWO
YOU CAN DO IT!
HOW TO ENACT STATE LITERACY LAW
by Richard Long

E very day almost fifty-four million children go to school. Some walk, some take the bus, some are driven. All arrive with a vast array of hopes, problems, challenges, assets, and potential, and as they move into their classrooms, they change from being individuals to part of a group. They are instructed as a group, yet it is as an individual that each learns—especially learning to read. Unfortunately, the system of teaching reading in groups leaves many people behind. When the instruction is poor or based on outmoded thinking, the entire class suffers. Even when the instruction is effective for many children, others are lost. Strong legislation is needed in each and every state to maximize each and every child's potential to learn and succeed. In this chapter we'll explore how to create laws that will work to close the educational gap, give teachers of reading the tools needed to be successful educators, and give every child the best chance to be well educated.

Form Your Idea

The first phase of an advocacy program, a call to action, is to develop an idea of what needs to be done; in this case, enacting a new state or local literacy law. With this goal in mind, a champion can be found to push your bill through a legislature into law. It also is the first step in finding allies who will help your champion win more attention and win votes.

Your bill is critically important. The bill is the actual fix for the problem. It addresses a wrong that you want to have righted. What will make or break your advocacy program is whether or not the bill is appealing to more than one person. This means that when a problem is so highly defined that it is about just a very few people, it will be very hard to rally others to your cause. In your case, the problem is about kids and good literacy skills. Literacy failure needs to be defined so that others can develop a stake in the problem and become willing to help fix it. Clearly state your idea—literacy law so all kids read—or it won't attract any others to promote it. Your "fix" can also be stated like this: Schools must teach all children who aren't learning to read using the best methods possible. What makes it gather strength is when others see their own children as having the same problem. The clarity of the idea is important because it moves people from the problem to the solution.

It is important to take your idea for change, new literacy law, and see what research has been done on the subject to determine how many children may be suffering from a similar problem and what happens to these children as a result. Seeking a legislative remedy will collapse if someone says, "Didn't we try to do something like this a few years ago?" or "Didn't we look into this a few years ago and find out that only a few people really have this problem?" Checking to see what data may be available in your state is critically important. How can you get this done?

First, an Internet search for your state is a good start. Second, find out if any literacy legislation has been introduced that has tried to deal with this problem, what was done as a result, and who were the organizers of the effort. Your members of Congress or their staff can help you locate the information. In addition, you can get help locally from teachers or administrators who would like to jump on your bandwagon because they want change, too.

Find a Champion

Finding the champion is more than just finding a friend who will listen and give advice. It means finding a state or local legislator or columnist who will take on the issue of literacy failure in public schools—the problem and the solution—as theirs. There are several ways to find a champion. One way is to meet with all the legislators who work on education in your city or state and see if there is any interest among the group. Another is to look into the backgrounds of all the legislators and see who has children or grandchildren in school. All parents, whether your next-door neighbor or a member of Congress, want their children to do well in school and will get very frustrated when they aren't getting the information or help they need for them to be successful.

Now that the background information is in hand, ask the appropriate members for an appointment to see them. Do bring information about your child/grandchild/friend's child—the problem, how many others it affects, and what needs to be done. Avoid raising the subject of the legislator's child, as this may feel like an intrusion on privacy. He or she has already made a decision as to how public to go with the child's problem.

Sometimes a legislator is looking for an issue that will make him a leader in the eyes of his colleagues and the wider community, even if he doesn't have a personal stake in the issue. Finding a champion based on an idea that may be appealing to him or her requires a little work. You can find out which members have already taken up similar causes in education, reading, prisons, welfare, etc. This is important, as rarely can a member of Congress be seen as the champion of too many causes, so he or she may "specialize" in some aspect of education and educational effects. Frequently, some of the best champions are fairly new to the legislative arena and have served for only one or two terms, but they have learned that fellow legislators hold knowledgeable colleagues in high regard, and they want to build their reputations. Literacy is a great place to start.

However, having a champion isn't enough. You need to help your champion build allies, using your call to action. Sometimes the allies come before choosing the champion. To find allies, you need to talk to others—start with other parents, and then talk to other community leaders and elected leaders. Don't be afraid to ask if they will help you. If a leader doesn't want to be your key leader or champion, he or she will say so. When this happens, he or she might say, "I will help, but I have a lot of other things on my plate," and offer a different way of helping out. Ask if you can count on him or her to vote for the bill if it comes up. Ask for advice about who is important in the legislative process for you to talk with. It is important to find out what the "natural" network is for your idea.

The Formal Process

In civics class you learned how the government works. Unfortunately, for most teenagers this wasn't their finest hour. However, it is important to understand how the formal process operates and the best time to intervene in it. Voters elect representatives who vote in bodies—legislatures at the state level and councils at the city level. The sequence of events is as follows: Ideas are introduced in a bill, and then they are studied by a committee of the legislature, voted out of committee, and then voted on by one chamber (for example, the state's House, Assembly, or the Senate) of a legislature. The next step is to work through the same sequence in the second chamber. After each chamber finishes a bill, the differences between the chambers then have to be resolved in what is called a conference committee. Finally, the bill is signed by the executive— the governor in a state or the president at the federal level. Simple.

One of the key links in this process is the agenda-setting role of the committee chairperson. The committee chairperson becomes the first filter in the formal legislative process. Once an idea is introduced and becomes a bill, the committee chairperson must decide if it will go forward. This decision is made based on the support the bill may have, as reflected by the members of the committee. You can help to get this crucial support by spending time briefing committee members to win their votes. This is done by setting up appointments and taking a copy of the draft legislation (www.state-literacy-law.org), the literacy bill, with examples of how the problem affects the committee member's district, his or her constituents' schools, or any other information that will help connect the committee member to your issue. Remember—you can more easily get support if people are attracted to the issue.

Your goal is to have committee members co-sponsor the legislation. This will send a signal to other members that there is strong support for the proposed literacy bill, because the more members who sign on as co-sponsors, the more strength and importance the bill has. One of the keys to seeking support and co-sponsorship is having members of both major political parties signed on as co-sponsors. Having bipartisan co-sponsors is one way of telling a committee chairperson that the literacy bill has the attention of the members.

Another way to get the chairperson's support is to ask for it directly. When a chairperson co-sponsors a bill, this is a powerful sign that he or she is in favor of it. To do this effectively, you need to find the support of others in the chairperson's home district.

This is how a bill becomes a law:

1. Bill is introduced
2. Committee hearing
3. Floor action
4. Other chamber—bill introduced
5. Committee hearing
6. Floor action
7. Conference committee
8. Signed into law

The Informal Process

The informal process of taking an idea and making it a law includes all the elements of the formal process but with one addition—by mustering the energy, compassion, or attention of lawmakers at each level of government, you can kick the formal process into high gear. Sometimes the informal system pushes the formal system through compelling testimony by a parent at a committee hearing.

Members of the legislature are frequently captivated not only by information in a presentation, but also by the pain with which parents talk about the needs of their children. This personal testimony that takes the issue to a human level makes a powerful impression and argument, one that members will sometimes quote during formal consideration of a measure.

Visit Your Lawmaker's Office

Visits to a member's office also make a strong impression. Most legislators maintain offices in their home district and in the capital. To find out about them, check the Internet site of your legislator or the online directory in the state government section. Call and ask for an appointment. Once the appointment is made, keep it, come on time, and bring information that is helpful to clarify your points on literacy failure in your/their schools. After saying hello, feel free to ask questions of your legislator with regard to their education knowledge (see Chapter Six for examples), then get quickly to the point and make it as clear as possible without making disparaging remarks. Let the facts speak for themselves. After you have presented these facts, ask for questions and don't be surprised by the questions you get. Remember, you have been living with this issue, but the legislator is just finding out about it. Always be polite, but ask for a commitment or for suggestions for what can be done.

Frequently, legislators will respond by saying that the first step will be a letter they will send asking for clarification of the issue from the responsible agency or individual, like the state school board or state secretary of education. If many children share the problem of learning to read, then a solution is needed. Ask for it.

Call into Action Your Lawmakers

Phone calls are another important tool to communicate with legislators, and the rules for communicating effectively hold here as well. Stay on task. Write down the points you want to make so you can follow them during the course of the conversation. You will be surprised that you can forget to ask for help or get caught up talking about some hurt or person who has treated you badly, rather than staying focused on the problem at hand. Make sure you are polite and listen, but don't forget you are asking for their help.

Write and Email Your Lawmakers

You and your team may be unable to visit your legislator in person, but you can send a letter or an email. Letters to members of a legislature need to have several critical points. First they need to be clear, state the problem (all children need to be taught to read), and make a request for action (we need a literacy law in our state or district). Don't send a letter with more than one issue in it. Don't threaten anyone. Threats rarely invite people to solve problems, and once you make a threat, any hope of discussion is over. Find the address of your legislator on the Web or in a phone book. Address any elected official as "The Honorable" ("The Honorable Jill Smith," for example). Examples of letters are presented in Chapter Six. State who you are and why you are writing. Be specific as to what you want done (a literacy law). Letters can also be a great way to communicate with more than one member of the legislature. They can provide individual lawmakers with background information about what the problem is and why your proposed solution makes sense.

Letters to the Editor

Most political offices have staff members responsible for reviewing letters to the editor that appear in the lawmaker's hometown newspapers to get an advance warning of problems his or her constituents are facing. If you want to raise attention about your issue, consider writing a letter to the editor of your local paper that responds to an article that appeared very recently in the paper on a related topic such as education, illiteracy, high school dropout rates, or prison populations. The letter should be brief and to the point, and either refute or agree with the points in the original article. Send your letter no more than two or three days after the original article, as it becomes old news after that time.

Don't Be Afraid to Compete

The legislative process is competitive. For every person who wants money spent one way, there are others who want it spent another way. And for each person who wants to change the status quo, there are others who want to keep things exactly as they are. Therefore, it is important to learn who may be opposed to literacy law and why.

The education field has a wide range of interest groups. Teachers, administrators, publishers, unions, politicians, and computer vendors all have their own special interests.

President Eisenhower, one of the nation's most respected presidents, had an interesting perspective on this. He never subscribed to the notion that those in opposition to his ideas were motivated by anything other than doing good. He avoided a lot of anger and focused on getting what he thought was the right thing done. He also did not give adversaries any fuel that could be used to complicate arguments to support his primary purpose. He talked about what needed to be done. You should do the same with literacy law.

But it's important to understand the perspective of your opposition. For teachers, it might mean the change you want will add to the demands of their day, or they don't have the training or the textbooks to teach a new way. They don't want to fail, either. For administrators, a new requirement might mean that funds are going in a direction they can't control, when they already have to cut back on things. For others, it may mean that a book series they worked on for ten years could become out of date. While it is important to understand what the barriers are, it is not a reason to stop pushing for vital change in literacy attainment.

To be successful in advocating for literacy law for your child and others, you need to understand that the legislative process involves people. Just like you and your allies, they had to start at the beginning to learn the process, and just like you, they have many pressures. It is hard not to take every setback as a slap in the face, but the reality is that the process is designed to be complex. The reason for this is simple: Our founding fathers did not want the government to pass laws too easily. They didn't trust government, so they wanted to make sure that it required a lot of agreement by many people to make a law. It is also a reason why it is important to always be polite. You never know when the person saying no to you today might be able to help in a small way later on in the process— remembering you as polite, yet forceful, may pay off down the road.

Taking the First Steps

Several years ago, a mother begged her fourth-grade son's teacher, "Please, just teach him to read." The teacher didn't know what to do. The mother asked the principal of the school why her children and others were not learning to read. The principal said it was complicated. At that point the mother went from pleading mother to advocate. This scene is played out in schools each day. When a parent is unable to achieve change in her child's school, she has two choices—to accept the limitations of the school and therefore sacrifice her child's future, or to seek a remedy elsewhere. And at this point, a parent steps into the role of state advocate.

Taking this step requires courage and conviction. It also requires persistence. It doesn't require lots of money, high-priced talent, or legions of movie stars standing in your corner. They are just tools. But you can use your voice and your determination to provide all children the best possible education and enlist groups of other parents to help move mountains. Others have done so over the last thirty years, and the result has been federal laws that require all schools to provide a quality education in the Elementary and Secondary Education Act; to allow children with disabilities to get a free, appropriate public education in the Education for All Handicapped Children Act; and to help struggling parents of poor families gain special help through the Title I program. These parents took their problems and turned them into ideas, and they found and recruited champions and allies by writing letters and making visits. They told their stories and, in doing so, helped not only their own children but also millions of other children. You can do the same for literacy in your state.

Just as women have redirected our medical research to address heart problems and breast cancer, and concerned parents have made a tremendous impact on drinking and driving laws, parents can also improve the reading education their children receive and, in doing so, help many others. If not parents, then who will speak for the children? Create your call to action, gather your allies, get the job done. It will be worth it.

Excerpted from Why Kids Can't Read: Challenging the Status Quo in Education, edited by Phyllis Blaunstein and G. Reid Lyon

CHAPTER THREE

AN ACTION PLAN FOR CONCERNED PARENTS AND CITIZENS

Yes, parents are committed to literacy and education for their children, grandchildren, and neighborhoods. And, yes, a call to action can offer families and communities the tools and the team to develop advocacy and civic skills.

"Why parent involvement? Parents do not perceive themselves as a constituency for children. They lack advocacy skills, but not the motivation or will to make change for children. The desire of parents to engage with purpose is impeded often by a lack of skill in how change comes about. Parents are rarely

encouraged to get past barriers to leadership
that are often seated in family history or
haunted by class, race, and gender bias. Your
call to action may be their first step in civic
skills. The cornerstones of true parent leader-
ship are respect, validation, and a belief that
when the tools of democracy are understood,
families will enter civic life."
—Elaine Zimmerman, Executive Director, Connecticut
Commission on Children

History shows us that community advocacy is *the* powerful force that can make possible any new law and for us, literacy law in your state. However, as with many industries and governments, education is a complicated, multilayered bureaucracy that needs to be understood.

One City's Story

Brownsville, Texas: One Community's Quest to
Turn Nonreaders into College-Bound Kids

Norma Garza's son, Alec, started having problems learning to read in first grade. By the age of ten, in fourth grade, he was still struggling to read. Desperate to get help for her son, Garza, who worked as an accountant, sought a diagnosis and guidance from a pediatric neurologist at the Texas Scottish Rite Hospital for Children in Dallas, Texas. It was the hospital staff who explained the importance of making education decisions based on science-based research as used in the medical field. Despite the fact that she had taken an analytical approach, read books on how children learned to read, and consulted national reading experts, Garza found that her son's public school was not only at a loss as to how to remedy the situation, but was pushing back against her suggestions and efforts. Garza joined forces with Elsa Cardenas-Hagen, a speech–language pathologist who owned a clinic for children with language and learning differences, in their hometown of Brownsville, Texas. They discussed the fact that the school district was providing only a computerized program that did not meet state standards for a dyslexia intervention program and that students in Brownsville were not being taught with a balanced approach to literacy, which would include phonological awareness, phonics, fluency, vocabulary, and comprehension skills.

Located on the U.S.-Mexico border, the Brownsville school district faced major hurdles, including poverty and a student population that is 98 percent Latino with few native English speakers. Such populations tend to have high numbers of children who fail to learn to read, as well as large numbers of students who drop out altogether. In 1996, Garza and Cardenas-Hagen co-founded the Brownsville Reads Task Force, a nonprofit organization of community members and educators who joined together to promote research-based reading instruction in the public and private schools of Brownsville, with the overall goal of creating a more literate community.

Together they created a strategic plan for the district that was approved by the school board, and Elsa personally retrained all kindergarten through third-grade teachers in a balanced approach for the development of Spanish literacy. Neuhaus Education Center in Houston, Texas, began collaboration with the school district to provide professional development in language enrichment (LE) via video conferencing, as it was not economical for teachers to travel to Houston for training, nor feasible to send Neuhaus staff to Brownsville. For the last fifteen years, with the help of Neuhaus, new teachers have been trained and refreshment trainings have been provided to current teachers, despite the district having had eight superintendents in the last fifteen years. This has helped to ensure continuity and sustainability.

Brownsville Reads began the initiative by working with regular education teachers in kindergarten through third grade. They then used Academic 2000 Goals money to retrain all teachers of dyslexic students and Title I funds to retrain upper elementary, middle school, and high school reading teachers, as well as English as a Second Language teachers. The Texas Reading Initiative provided further training, and the No Child Left Behind Act helped initiate Reading First. As Cardenas-Hagen explains, "You see, we were already using this model in the late 1990s because we improved our regular education literacy instruction, and only those students who were not responding to this multisensory, structured reading instruction were given extra instruction. Having trained reading coaches and mentors has been extremely helpful. This was made possible with the Reading First Grant."

During this time, the Brownsville school district also participated in research initiatives sponsored by the National Institutes of Health and the Institute for Education Sciences, led by the University of Houston and the University of Texas at Austin. "It is due to the research that we have been conducting in this district and other districts across the nation, that we have learned more about how to instruct English language learners and students who struggle with learning to read. Brownsville is on the cutting edge because it is the laboratory from which public policy will be set in the future," explains Cardenas-Hagen.

And, the results speak for themselves. According to Neuhaus: *After the first year of the initiative, a group of 522 second-grade students was identified. Half the students had been taught by teachers who had received the professional development; the other half had been taught by teachers who had not yet received the professional development. The achievement of the group on the state-mandated reading tests was followed from third through fifth grades. Students who had received LE instruction in second grade performed at statistically significantly higher levels of proficiency on the third-grade test than students in the other half of the group. Continued higher achievement of the students who had received LE in second grade was documented in an analysis of the fifth-grade test.*

Cardenas-Hagen and Garza believe this success can be recreated elsewhere, and they offer the following checklist of must-haves:

- A strategic plan of action
- Evidence-based decision-making procedures
- Data-validated intervention programs
- A strategic, professional development plan
- Support from business and community leaders
- Research within the district
- A plan for working with English language learners and students with reading difficulties (SEEDS)
- Mentors and coaches
- Fidelity of implementation
- Public policy at the local, state, and national level to support reading reform
- Financial resources
- A leadership sustainability plan for community systemic reform

SEEDS can learn to read despite economic and language barriers; our 90/90/90 schools continue to prove this all over the country. Brownsville is a stellar example of how concerned citizens and a very determined mother took charge. Brownsville is the perfect example of grassroots efforts within a community. Further, the Brownsville School District was awarded the Broad Prize for Urban Education in 2008, which offers $1 million in scholarships, allowing students the opportunity to go to college. Brownsville was able to successfully reverse the trend of illiteracy within one generation, truly leaving no child behind. More impressive, if anything could be in education, is that Brownsville's successes drove many more efforts in both Texas and around the country to ensure that students received science-based literacy instruction.

The Action Plan

When seeking to bring about change and improvement, how far do we need to go? Whom do we need to talk to? What do we need to ask for? When have we achieved victory? It is these questions that we hope to answer in this chapter.

As with everything in life, creating a simple action plan will help you work through your state education bureaucracy to make an impact. Following these steps helped in the quest to improve reading instruction in Texas and to move higher education law in Minnesota and dyslexia law in Texas. This is the basic plan:

1. Know the problem. As we said in Chapter One, you are seeking to solve the problem that too many kids in the state can't read well enough to comprehend their grade-level textbooks. How is this possible? Get the facts for your state.

2. Focus on the solution: a new literacy law for all students to be literate. This could be playfully called "research is your friend." Do your homework. Understand the issues. Who is for or against fixing the literacy problem? What are their positions? Why? Know the data. Be confident that the state has made a big mistake in how kids are taught to read and how teachers of reading are prepared to teach. This is not the student's fault. This is not the teacher's fault; but it is the system's fault. There is an opportunity to correct it; but first, you need for the state's bureaucracy to admit the problem, be willing to enact law that drives change, and be willing to spend the money necessary to fix it. This won't be easy.

3. Use the power of information to support your case. After you have consumed the information and data available to you, feed it to those who can make the decisions. This information is a powerful

tool to support your request for literacy law. Data shouldn't sit on a shelf; it should inform and guide policy and practical decision-making. Data-validated practices and professional development, instruction, and assessment are imperative for student success. As an example in California, despite the "best" core language curriculum available and a bevy of "trained" teachers, California students were almost at the bottom of the pack when it came to reading scores since the removal of phonics-based professional development and curriculums. In contrast, there are a few hundred 90/90/90 schools whose data prove that evidence-based reading instruction, along with universal screening, assessments, a multitier system of supports, and well-prepared teachers of reading, are a clear fix to the haphazard approach to reading instruction today. Now all California needs is new literacy legislation to ensure all schools follow suit.

4. Insist on moving toward enacting each component within the model literacy legislation. Don't accept "no" for an answer. The Minnesota team did not accept "no." They kept right on going until they enacted law for preparing emerging reading teachers in the universities and colleges of education. Why? Because of the obvious: Their colleges of education were not preparing new teachers of reading to teach to a diverse SEEDS students population, and the state's student achievement data were abysmal. There is always a way to keep the discussion going or to move this issue closer into the spotlight. Use retailing: Focus your selling point on the law to help it move toward becoming a reality. This is also the time to identify your allies and supporters and work with organizations and individuals who can help with the grassroots. A lone voice won't carry the day. You need more than a stack of papers and advice. You need to identify and recruit supporters in and out of politics, as discussed in Chapter One.

5. Overcome obstacles. Change isn't easy. But if you prepare for your opponents, the naysayers, and the protectors of the status quo, you can confront these obstacles and overcome them. Remember, that which is worth changing often isn't easy to change.

6. Push with all your might against all parties fighting the adoption of new literacy legislation. Ask them why they are against these important practices when student achievement facts are so stark. Keep your antennas tuned to both state and federal reports. When the NAEP examination is administered and reveals the same poor test scores year after year, you will have the ears of those making the decisions and possibly a few early opponents. When the Common Core State Standards can't be met, you and your team will be in demand and the research papers, once ignored, will be requested and read. They will listen to your experts. And, unanimously, they will ratify the legislation desperately needed for each student to succeed.

7. Tell a story about your state. As an example, let's think again about the $14 billion per year that California wastes on remedial college education. Then let's look at the state's largest school district, Los Angeles (LA) Unified (second largest in the U.S.), and its high school graduation rate. Then let's look at a few statistics, such as how much LA Unified spends per year per student. Fact: LA Unified spends more than $30,000 a year per student beginning in kindergarten. Think about that. That is more money per student toward tuition than the very best charter and private elementary and secondary schools; heck, it's more in tuition than most colleges and universities! One would think that the system's high school graduation rates would be high. Wrong. The high school graduation rate of LA Unified students is only 40.6 percent. Yes, this means that after spending $30,000 each year per student, nearly six in ten students will *not* graduate from high school. This also means that if a student can't read well enough to pass tenth grade and drops out, more than $330,000 has gone into this student's "dropout" education. This is criminal.

You can also tell a national story about the cost of not graduating U.S. teenagers from high school. According to the U.S Department of Education, the 1,230,000 students who drop out nationally each year cost the country $319 billion in lost wages, taxes, and productivity over their lifetimes. You can then deduce for LA Unified that each student dropout from the nation's second-largest school district costs $260,000 in lost wages, taxes, and productivity plus $330,000 in educational costs—almost $600,000. The numbers alone are hard to fathom; but more important than economic costs to society is how much we are robbing from these individuals, both physiologically and financially. The economic story is a powerful one to tell, though, as powerful as the prison inmate who learns to read while in prison and achieves a GED. It is possible that with reading literacy skills and a high school diploma, this person would never have been in prison to begin with.

Like anything else in life, these seven steps seem much easier in theory than they are in practice. Getting folks to work together is not always easy, but once started, it can be overwhelmingly rewarding. You need to trust us here. Change can happen, and you can achieve it.

> *"Culture does not change because we desire to change it. Culture changes when the organization is transformed; the culture reflects the realities of people working together every day."*
> —Frances Hesselbein, Leader to Leader

CHAPTER FOUR

FIRST HELPING MY CHILD, *THEN* CREATING COMMUNITY CHANGE

by Elenn Steinberg

The task of working to create systems change in literacy may appear like too much of a challenge—especially when dealing with the day-to-day struggles of how to help our own child survive in an educational world that is based on the ability to read. As parents, we ourselves struggle to navigate a system that doesn't seem to understand what to do with children (SEEDS) who have difficulty learning to read. While it is essential that we change these systems, often we are confronted by the overwhelming needs of our individual child.

While you instinctively know that the world of literacy must change, at this moment your primary focus must be procuring services for your child. Each child must successfully navigate through school and optimally thrive. However, we know that, generally speaking, when one child is not learning how to read, there are many more who are failing as well. Regardless of the various reasons for this, the job of the school is to teach *all* children to read, including the SEEDS students.

As the parent with the child who is struggling, the task of working with the school can be daunting. We may feel as if we are confronting our own past as we tuck ourselves into the desk or small chair we remember from years ago. In order to help our own children succeed, we must step outside of our school experience, build our own understanding of the system that now exists for our child, and press on. When working with a school, assume the best. Teachers genuinely want to teach children so that they may succeed in school and in life. However, teachers don't know what they don't know, so it may be up to parents and guardians to help guide them.

Surviving the System

So where does a family member start to ensure that his or her child's needs are met at school?

The best place to start is at home. Spend time organizing your thoughts about your child's educational experience, successes, and challenges. Identify your concerns. Be specific and go into detail. Only you can know what goes on at home and when a child is struggling. A parent can bring insight to the situation that the school may be missing.

Details about reading may include the areas of language in which he or she struggles. If he or she is not able to sound out words, guessing words very slowly, or showing a lack of comprehension, make notes—as this is the place to begin. Other examples that only you can know may include that your child spends an excessive amount of time on homework compared to his or her peers. Only you know that he or she cries at the end of the day, voicing that he or she feels like a failure, or whether he or she feigns illness to avoid turning in incomplete homework or feeling unprepared to take an exam. You may know about the teacher who calls your child lazy or tells him or her to work harder—when you know that your child does work hard, but without success. Take time to learn about dyslexia and how children learn to read so that you can come to school armed with facts. This can also include past reports from teachers or professional assessment data, although those are not required. Further, ready yourself with details on how your child is doing in other subjects, as writing and math can be equally troublesome for some kids.

The Meeting

Request a meeting with your child's teacher. Determining the goals that you want to accomplish at this meeting will help determine who should be at the meeting. Can the classroom teacher accomplish the goals, or do you need to include the principal, reading specialist, or special-education teacher? Special-education service administrators can provide you with the documents you need to sign to have assessments done. This also puts them, by law, on the clock to accomplish this result. Check your state department of education's website to determine the time frame for this to be accomplished, because while this falls under the Individuals with Disabilities Act (IDEA) special-education law and is mandatory, states can set their own timelines. More information on the American Disabilities Act (ADA) and Individuals with Disabilities Education Act (IDEA) federal law is available in the Model Literacy Law (available at www.state-literacy-law.org).

You can start the conversation by simply saying, "My child doesn't seem to be reading (writing, spelling, doing math) very well." Provide the details you have prepared on what your child is struggling with: sound, fluency, spending too much time on homework, dislikes reading, reports to "hate school," is depressed, compares him or herself to other students, or feels like a failure.

Bring examples of his or her work to help demonstrate the marginal spelling or other academic struggles. Share the stories that your student brings home about being shamed by a teacher who singles him or her out for his or her challenges. Share anecdotes and stories that move the people in the room to feel compassionately about your child. And finally, ask if your child could be a SEEDS student (Struggling readers, English language learners, Economically disadvantaged youth, students with Dyslexia and Specific learning disabilities). States, schools, and school districts use different nomenclature for kids who struggle with reading. The words "dyslexia" and "learning disability," however, are the terms used in federal law. Special education law lists them as a specific learning disability [20 U.S.C. 1401 (30)]. Be sure to state your goal—your child reading and succeeding—and then discuss what services might be the most appropriate to accomplish said goal.

Being a SEEDS student or having dyslexia will not automatically qualify a child for special services. The qualifications for special-education services are defined by the district and require assessment data, which differs from state to state. At this time, most states have implemented a program called either Response to Intervention (RtI) or Multitier System Supports (MTSS), as noted in the Model State Literacy Law, which can be highly beneficial since they provide immediate services for any child who is determined to be at risk. These services are provided according to data gathered in your child's class. The teacher is responsible for regular evaluations to ensure all students are learning at grade level. These assessments are standardized and not conjecture on the part of the teacher. One popular and excellent assessment tool is called *Dibels Next* and it can be viewed online so you have an idea of what the assessment looks like. Children in older grades may use benchmark assessments that show where a child is in comparison to the standards for that grade statewide or even nationally. While useful, this information may not tell you how your child is performing in the key components of reading—phonological awareness, phonics, comprehension, and vocabulary. Additionally, the school staff should have work samples that demonstrate the success and challenges your child faces. However, you, as the parent, can still request an assessment for special education regardless of the Multitier System of Supports (MTSS) plan a school may have in place, as that is your right under the Individuals with Disabilities Act (IDEA).

In the course of the conversation, you might want to ask these questions to assess if your school offers the tools your child will need:

- How do you teach reading in this school?
- Do you use any particular programs?
- Does the school have a core reading instruction program? Is it utilizing multi-component, structured language instruction?
- How are you identifying and assessing students at risk?
- What is the intervention program and tiered supports the school is using to support SEEDS?
- How are you identifying students at risk in your MTSS model (see information below)?
- What type of professional development has the school been providing to staff to educate them on teaching reading effectively?
- Keep all the information you collect in a file so that if you need to follow up, you have all the information necessary to demand more support for your child.

This then becomes a series of if/then questions. *If* they take your concerns seriously, *then* request a time line so you can track what is happening and what results are being produced. This should be at least every two weeks and not longer than three.

If they are providing MTSS services, *then* you want to know how they track progress and how they will be reporting to you.

I'd suggest email if that is possible, as it is quick and easy for all involved. Report card periods are often not frequent enough!

If the services they provide your child work, *then* you applaud and continue to follow up with monitoring progress on a regular basis. (This can be every two weeks in some situations—it should not be longer than four weeks and gains should be strong and consistent.)

If your child is not making adequate gains, *then* you must request assessment for special education. Do not wait longer than six weeks even if the school requests this—your child is now six weeks further behind!

If they are doing assessment for special-education services, *then* you need to be given a time line so you can be prepared for the follow-up meeting, which will be within forty-five to sixty days from the time you provided permission to assess. Be sure to check your school system's website for the laws in your state. At that point, you need to understand what it takes to have your child become a grade-level reader. Four simple keys are listed in the Model Literacy Law: 1) structured, systematic, multi-component teaching; 2) a well-trained, highly skilled teacher of reading; 3) adequate time and support; and 4) intensity of instruction.

A Bit More

The Individuals with Disabilities Education Act (IDEA) protects the rights of *all* children under the law. You can request an assessment for special education for your child at any time, even within an MTSS model. However, special education does not guarantee that your child will be provided a highly skilled, certified teacher of reading who is able to teach him or her to read. It is important to understand what it takes to catch a child up to where he or she needs to be to keep up with classmates.

If, after speaking with your child's teacher and principal, you feel you have not received a satisfactory response to your questions and a request for intervention, your next step is to go up the ladder. Contact the district's or area's special-education director as listed on the district or state website and research services for individuals or parental support organizations. Federal law mandates each of these offices in every state, and they are available to you as a resource.

You are your child's best advocate. Keep pushing until you get the answers you need and your child gets the help that he or she is entitled for a successful educational experience.

Can a Parent Influence Change on a School System?

Parents have the ability to create change in schools, though often it does not appear that way. While one parent can create awareness, multiple parents can work together to move mountains. Talk to other parents, attend a PTA meeting, network, and gather people and resources that will be useful. Set up a meeting with the principal. In some cases, providing the principal with the facts you have gathered and a sample of the Model Literacy Law we have created and demonstrating how the changes you want for the school will benefit not just your child but *all* children, could be just what it takes to bring about that change. In other cases, you may face more of a challenge, so you need to be tenacious, engaged, and committed, as stated in Chapter One of this book.

Here are some larger issues you may want to address. They are the primary reasons we ask everyone to join the call to action to enact literacy law in every state in the country:

- How do you teach failing readers, all SEEDS kids?

- How does your state certify teachers of reading? Does the exam include questions that address the phonological system of our language, fluency, comprehension, expressive vocabulary, semantics, and critical thinking skills?
- What is your state doing about the high number of failing readers?
- How does the state certify teachers of reading?
- How does the state monitor teacher quality and student achievement?
- How does the state monitor teacher education programs to ensure that graduates effectively teach reading to all students, including our SEEDS students?

Partnerships Are Important—Don't Go It Alone

You can form grassroots partnerships with others in your community, as Cinthia Coletti Haan describes in Chapter One. Form these partnerships with those having similar concerns and work together. Groups to cultivate as allies include the following:

- Parents
- Teachers of reading
- Educators
- Administrators
- Psychologists
- Pediatricians
- Minority organizations
- Community associations—small business, youth, after school
- State departments of education

- School boards—national and state associations of school boards, principals, superintendents
- Parents and teachers associations—state PTA boards
- Learning disability schools
- Education groups—special education, twice-exceptional
- Teachers' unions
- International Reading Association
- Learning Disabilities Association
- National Center for Learning Disabilities
- University and college support services offices
- Gifted-student groups
- Children and adults with attention deficit and hyperactive disorders; attention deficit support group

Do not let what you cannot do interfere with what you can do.

—Ancient Chinese Proverb

CHAPTER FIVE

A MOTHER'S MESSAGE FOR YOU AND YOUR CALL TO ACTION

Dear Moms, Dads, Grandparents, Colleagues, and Friends:

I highly support the effort for new state literacy law. The parent on the front line, whether or not his or her child struggles to read, slightly or mightily, the teacher in the classroom, the administrators in the schools, the businessperson who wants a talented workforce, the citizens who pay taxes—all want for *all* children to be taught effectively for the reasons that are important to them. To focus on only the neediest students is divisive and slow, and it allows hundreds of thousands of kids to continue to fall off the cliff each year, with slim, if not unattainable, chances of reaching the summit of reading proficiency.

I say this as the mother of a twenty-two-year-old son with dyslexia. I worked closely with teachers and administrators in his schools, developing respectful partnerships. As hard as I tried, even as a school board member who had educated herself over many years, given the school staff's limited knowledge about reading development, I failed to get enough people to listen, understand, and act in ways that would effectively help my son and other students in the school. They thought my son was different from their struggling readers at home and in the classroom.

Remember, the average person, whether he or she is a parent, teacher, or government official, does not understand the issues of struggling readers and will not dive into the mud—who has the time? Parents are trying to raise a family and pay the bills; teachers can't wait for summer as they struggle, too, teaching twenty-five to thirty kids with little support and ineffective professional development; and lawmakers are negotiating, compromising, and writing laws while posturing to get reelected.

This is an issue that affects *all* of us through increased health costs, economic loss, diminished intellectual contributions, increased societal costs, entitlement programs, prisons and local law enforcement, and, most devastating, the psychological costs to the individuals and their families. The wisdom I have gained over time compels me to see that this is an issue of reading equity and reading potential for all. We need literacy laws in every state in this nation.

I pray, with great respect to all of you who are working so hard, so passionately to change things, and most likely joined this journey because dyslexia, limited English proficiency, or functional illiteracy has touched your children: *Please* know that to correct this injustice, this violation of science and civil rights, we *must* focus, *all* of us—child, teenager, adult, rich, poor, black, white, brown, yellow—on whether we read well or not at all. This issue is a call for education reform to ensure all kids are taught to read.

Just so you know, my son is doing great—after lots of money and time. He did get remediation and education but outside the public schools. He has become and will continue to be a successful adult.

Sincerely,

Cheryl Ward, MS, AALT
President, Wisconsin Branch, International
Dyslexia Association

CHAPTER SIX

TOOLBOX AND COOKBOOK FOR READING LITERACY

This chapter will provide you with the tools and ingredients to embark upon your call to action. Together with Rich Long and Elenn Steinberg, we have assembled key topics and the critical communication tools you will need. In this chapter, I will share sample communications and messaging, research, and statistics to quote based on focus group findings. You also will find a script for engaging people in the grassroots effort to enact literacy law. It is important to know if your state has signed onto the Common Core State Standards Initiative (Standards). If it has, weave in the fact that achieving the Standards is not possible without reading literacy and that Literacy Law will ensure student success in the Standards:

> The Standards set requirements not only for English language arts (ELA) but also for literacy in history, social studies, science, technology and new media subjects. The

Standards are the culmination of an extended, broad-based effort to fulfill the charge issued by the states to create the next generation of K–12 standards in order to help ensure that all students are college and career ready in literacy no later than the end of high school.[19]

Political Engagement—Ask Questions

It is first important to know as much as possible about your local politicians before you meet with them. But don't be so busy learning that you don't get to the "doing." As Stephen Smith adeptly states in his book, *Stoking the Fire of Democracy*, "Instead of wondering what may persuade our targets, we summoned the courage to ask them." Ask them about their top priority and why it is important to them. Ask them what legislation they are most proud of enacting. Ask them about their feelings on the state of education. This will help you understand their points of reference and develop a dialogue so you can engender understanding. This will also prevent you from making the often-fatal mistake of a one-way feed of information. After establishing a bit of conversation, you can move into a series of more personal questions before you present your facts and request their support.

Focus groups found the following conversational questions potent:

1. *"When your children (grandchildren) were growing up, did they want to learn to read and go to school? Can you recall them learning how to read? Have you ever known a young child who did not want to learn to read and graduate from high school?"* These questions summon the imagery of their children or grandchildren taking those necessary

---

19 National Governors Association Center for Best Practices and the Council of Chief State School Officers, Introduction, Common Core State Standards, citing website http://www.corestandards.org/assets/CCSSI_ELA%20Standards.pdf (accessed September 12, 2011).

first steps—steps that took work; steps that are not natural; steps that needed to be taught. And, of course, all kids want to read and succeed in school. Remember to say that we fail to teach children to read; they don't fail us.

2. *"Can you share with me what happens to the neighborhood students that dropout of high school, unable to read their textbooks, unable to pass their classes?"* Yes, they know the answer: Characteristically, the recourse for these students is social services, crime, or both.

3. You can also ask curious questions for which they may not know the answers: *"Did you know that only X percent of our state's kids read at grade level in the eighth grade? What do you think will happen to these local students who can't read at grade level? If these statistics continue and they drop out of high school, what will happen to our state's GSP?"* Use the NAEP eighth-grade reading score for your state. Trust me, the scores won't be high and should instigate compelling recognition for why you are meeting with them. Small, concrete numbers can be very effective. For example, "Only three out of ten students in our state can read proficiently!"

4. And, the last and most important question is *"As our state representative, can you allow this crisis to continue for another day unchallenged?"* At this point they can identify with the problem and recognize that they can't allow it to continue. Next, they will want a solution and hope that you have one.

Now that you have gained their agreement that the literacy failure problem is serious and cannot continue, you can politely ask them to help solve the problem by championing state literacy law—by being a leader. Ask for their commitment to adopt the issue of literacy failure as their own. Ask if they will meaningfully get the issue on the next agenda, move the bill through the committee, and make certain the bill is enacted into literacy law.

Once you have had your first meeting, feel proud. Recap the meeting with your team and get their feedback. Talk to them about how it felt to be in the room with your state assemblyperson. Share the answers given to your questions. Talk about what went well and what needs more work. Fine-tune your presentation after each and every meeting. Then. prepare your next steps: follow-up letters, phone calls, emails, requests, and schedules for your next series of meetings. Tweet, blog, and listserv this information to everyone you can in the state. Get others to do the same. Our state representatives, I am assured, pay close attention to the "social voices" of their constituents. When you can get hundreds of "networkers" tweeting away, things happen very quickly.

Tools to Turn the Tide

Master the statistics and ask questions to turn the tide in your direction. A one-way feed seldom produces agreement. Use questions to get all parties involved in thinking and responding. Listen to their views. Stick with the facts and use "sculpted language" that challenges the status quo. Do not lose sight of the goal.

Focus groups responded enthusiastically and with affirming ratings to the following questions and statistics about education issues. Use these examples confidently to empower your advocacy. Communicate with your representatives regularly and universally in your campaign, and remember to elicit their feelings, emphasize equality, use imagery, and play the American card of exceptionalism.

1. Your statement: *"Statistics show "American fifteen-year-olds rank fifteenth out of thirty-four developed countries in reading literacy"* (OECD, 2009).

Your question: *"Why do you think America is falling behind so many other countries?" Wait for the answer, then ask, "What can we do about it?"*

This statement/question dialogue has a sense of the personal and the exceptional: How can this be? Aren't we the best?

2. Your statement: *"The statistics show an incomprehensible forty-two million Americans cannot read, write, or perform simple math. Another fifty million Americans cannot read past the fourth-grade level"* (National Right to Read Foundation).

Your question: *"How do you think people support themselves and their families if they can't read?"* *Wait for the answer, then ask, "Do you think it is more difficult to be functionally illiterate in today's advancing twenty-first century than in the past century?"*

This question projects vivid good imagery of inequality, social failure, and sadness about feeling left behind in today's tech-driven society.

3. Your statement: *"The statistics show less than three in ten of America's eighth-grade public school students meet the NAEP standard of reading proficiency"* (NCES, 2009).

Your question: *"If this is true, and I believe it is, what do you think it means for 70 percent of my neighborhood kids that I see walking to school each day?"* *Wait for the answer, then ask, "What do you think the future for these children looks like?" and "What does it mean for our country?"*

This question brings to mind the kids in his or her neighborhood—it makes the issue personal, shows inequality, and has good imagery.

4. Your statement: *"The statistics show about two in three prison inmates are high school dropouts and one in three were also juvenile offenders that read well below the fourth-grade level."* (Haynes, 2007).

Your question: *"Did you know the local high school district is only graduating x percent of my hometown kids?"* *Wait for the acknowledgement, then ask, "What will these kids do? Go on social services? Turn to crime? What do you think?"*

These questions inspire a sense of urgency while again stressing the inequality of the situation.

5. Your statement: The statistics show *"30 percent of all public school students do not graduate from high school"* (NCES, 2008) *and that "more than three out of four people on welfare are illiterate"* (Washington Literacy Council).

<u>Your question</u>: *"Can you tell me how we are going to support sixteen million of our fifty-four million public school children who will not graduate from high school?"* *Wait for the answer, then ask,* *"Does it astonish you?"* *Wait...* *"What does it mean—higher taxes, more prisons, drug cartels?"* *Wait...* *"What is your plan?"*

These questions all pose good imagery, give a sense of the personal, establish the need for equality, and call for the legislator to assume responsibility and take action.

Focus groups concluded that these five statement/questions get the attention of legislators and the American people. Following this process puts the listener in a position where he or she will feel compelled to respond—at a minimum with an opinion, and, if you're successful, with a commitment to take responsibility. Be sure to arm yourself and your allies with these five impactful statistics and questions to use in your call to action and social marketing campaigns.

Research that Resonates

This section provides reading research on third-grade literacy failure and its correlation to high school dropout rates. Keep this information readily available in your toolbox. Memorize these facts, if possible, and especially have them handy if you get nervous and are asked a question. Our goal is to have all incoming fourth-grade students reading literate so they can begin to learn subject material. Numerous studies speak to the fact that grade-level reading proficiency by third grade is compulsory for educational attainment through postsecondary.

During your meetings, continue to highlight for your legislators and grassroots teams the importance of student literacy—the earlier the better, but it is never too late for any student to become reading literate. Ultimately, share with your champion(s) that we know this requires a process of retraining, retooling, testing, certifying, and supporting our teachers of reading, reading specialists, and content area teachers so they can best serve the diverse needs of their students. Support your goal by saying, *"This responsibility is made most clear when we focus on the correlation of third-grade reading skills and students that drop out of high school. Much of what these studies show is that future teen drug use and violence in high school point to the fact these students are frustrated because they seriously struggle with reading and, thus, passing their classes. Psychologically they feel academically helpless. We are robbing them of a future if we don't teach them to be reading literate."* Insist upon certified and qualified teachers of reading in every classroom—to include all prekindergarten to third-grade classroom teachers and specialists in reading, English Language Learners (ELL), Title I, and special education in grades four through twelve, and all content area teachers who teach reading.

Here are specific questions to ask parents and members of your community to gain grassroots support, as well as the sustaining research to cite so you can achieve community cohesiveness:

1.QUESTION: *"Is your third-grade child (grandchild) reading well?" "Did you know that students reading below the proficient range in third grade are not likely to graduate from high school?"*

FACTS: Students reading below the proficient range in third grade are not likely to graduate from high school.

The research shows that a child's reading proficiency by third grade has a direct correlation to his or her success in high school and beyond. Effectively, reading does matter by the end of third grade and there is a strong link between third grade reading skill and high school dropout rates.

Sources: (1) Study and report issued in April 2008 on high school graduation rates: *Cities in Crisis: A Special Analytic Report on High School Graduation*, Christopher B. Swanson, Ph.D., of the EPE Research Center, supported by America's Promise Alliance and the Bill and Melinda Gates Foundation. (2) *Becoming a Nation of Readers: The Report of the Commission on Reading*, Anderson, Hiebert, Scott, and Wilkinson. (1985). (3) *Developmental Lag Versus Deficit Models of Early Reading Disability: A Longitudinal, Individual Growth Curves Analysis*, Francis, Shaywitz, Stuebing, Shaywitz, and Fletcher, *Journal of Educational Psychology*, Vol. 88. No. 1, 1996.

2. QUESTION: *"Do you know why reading is so important to your child's education?"*

Research shows that with the current state of reading instruction in our country, we can expect the following: If a child is reading poorly at the end of first grade, chances are high that he or she will read poorly at the end of fourth grade and, further, if he or she is still reading poorly in ninth grade, there is a high probability that he or she will drop out of high school.

Research demonstrates that "88 percent of youngsters who read poorly at the end of the first grade read poorly at the end of the fourth grade, as well. Students who have not caught up by nine years of age carry their limited reading skills into adulthood. For those students who have not learned to read by the ninth grade, these youths typically drop out of school at significantly higher rates than their classmates who read proficiently."

Sources: (1) Alliance for Excellent Education (2008) *The High Cost of School Dropouts*. (2) *What's Gone Wrong in America's Classrooms* (pp. 49–90). Stanford, CA: Hoover Institution Press (Evers). (3) *Reading: A Research-Based Approach* (Fletcher, J. M., and Lyon, G. R.) 1998. (4) *Preventing Reading Difficulties in Young Children*. Washington, DC: National Academy Press (Snow, Burns, and Griffin), 1998.

Sample Letter to Your Legislator

You will be surprised to know that a well-thought-out letter is still one of the most effective ways Americans have of influencing lawmakers. Many of us today use email to communicate; however, do not underestimate the power of a signed letter from a constituent. If email is easier, attach the letter to the email as a document file .

First, keep the letter simple, direct, and polite—one page, if possible. Let the recipient know right away why you are writing— the problem—and write with a "sense of the personal." Say who you are (include that you are a voter in his or her district, as well as your credentials and follow-up address). Provide factual details. If a legislative bill is involved, cite the correct title or number. Close your letter asking for specific action on their part (for example, to support new state literacy law).

Second, know the protocol for addressing your letter by understanding the workings of your state legislative body. This information is readily available on the state's website. It is important to address the letter correctly: The Honorable [insert first and last name]. Make sure you specifically address the correct body of the legislature (for example, City Council, State Assembly, and State Legislature) and use the correct salutation for your state representative depending on the office held (Dear Assemblyman [insert last name]. Other examples include Congresswoman, Senator, and Representative).

Sample Letter/Email To A Legislator

The Honorable Trisha Gates
Nevada State Assembly
State Capitol, Room 401
Carson City, NV 89701

Dear Assemblywoman Gates,

I am writing to ask for your support to end literacy failure in our classrooms. As a citizen, I feel strongly that our schools should, at the very least, teach all students to be literate. I read in the newspaper that my school district, is graduating only 40 percent of its high school students. This means that 60 percent of these students are dropping out of high school into our community with little or no opportunity for the future. I have learned that a leading cause of these children dropping out of school is their inability to read grade-level textbooks, without which they cannot pass their classes. This has me worried for my family, my neighborhood, my town, and our state. We really can't allow this to happen, and we need your help to make a dramatic change to fix this problem.

I am a family man, a Nevada citizen, and a small business owner living at 2401 Top Valley Road, Reno, Nevada. Two of my three children are having a hard time reading and are falling behind in their other subjects. So many others in their schools are suffering with the same problem. Based on the statistics, my wife and I are afraid they will drop out of school. We need your help.

I am writing to request that you do everything in your power to fix this reading problem so our kids are taught to read and write, so they can fulfill their promise and follow their dreams. I have learned that there is a potential new Nevada law on literacy that will fix this problem. Please do all you can to pass this law for my children and our community's children.

Thank you for your consideration,

John McInerney Garcia
2401 Top Valley Road
Reno, NV 89503
JMG@gmail.com
(702) 555-3172

SAMPLE EMAIL TO THE EDITOR

Letters to an editor are best emailed but can also be mailed. Keep it to the point and be witty and succinct. It is best if you are responding to an article that was in the paper or magazine that involves education. If so, mention the article right away. Be focused on your message. Write no more than two or three paragraphs. First, introduce your problem (literacy failure/high school dropouts) and your objective (all students literate—first/new state literacy law). Support your view. Include your name, address, affiliation(s), email address, and phone number so they can contact you to verify your authorship of the letter. You may ask that your information be withheld from publication.

Dear Dayton Daily News:

Today's article in your paper, "Finding Qualified Employees," got my heart racing. How in the world can our schools graduate students who can't read, write, or spell? I was recently traveling to Japan to stay with friends. Did you know that the majority of Japanese students graduate from college and become productive citizens, earning a paycheck and paying taxes?

America is losing its grip and in a few more generations may not be able to compete in the world's economy. If, according to OECD, American fifteen-year-olds finished fifteenth out of twenty-one developed countries in literacy, it won't take too long before the U.S. reaches the bottom. Then what?

I have heard that many states are enacting literacy laws that require teachers of reading to learn the best methods that ensure all students learn to read, write, spell, and think about what they are reading. As so many other states are out-producing Ohio in literacy, maybe it is time for your paper to raise public awareness and make a push to enact new state literacy law for Ohio. This way we can graduate students who are able to enter the workforce and raise families without going on welfare.

Yours truly, wanting the best for our state and country,

John G. Morgan
Retired Naval Officer
2509 Seminary Drive
Akron, OH 44301
Email: oldcutter@aol.com
Phone: 330-572-8878

SAMPLE DIALOGUE FOR ENLISTING GRASSROOTS TEAM MEMBERS

When you recruit folks to join your efforts, all the components of Chapter One come into play. You want to be direct, honest, and forthright in your expression about your mission. Create a sense of the personal, use equality, and invoke imagery. You will be most effective if you present the problem with the results-driven solution, motivate them to understand that action can solve the problem, and ultimately ask them to join you in ending the status quo and challenging the education system to be better for all students and America's future.

SAMPLE SCRIPT

Hello,

I want to talk to you about the reading crisis in our school. Did you know that more than 70 percent of our eighth-grade students can't read their textbooks proficiently?

We've embarked on a grassroots effort across the state to tackle this problem this year. We've talked to teachers, principals, parents, children, and community and business leaders. In short, we have done our homework and have a plan to fix the problem of our kids not learning to read in our schools. This plan can have impact, starting in year one. What we are doing to our kids' future is immoral:

- Without the ability to read, our students drop out of high school and have nowhere to turn but crime, prison, drugs, and social dependency. We can change this, year one.
- We need genuine accountability so that every tax dollar goes to educate students, not support bureaucracies that

are robbing our kids of a future through illiteracy. We can change this, year one.

- With a new state literacy law for our school, we can ensure that all kids learn to read. We can make it happen this year.

We don't need your money. But we need your commitment and a few minutes of your time.

Imagine how proud you will be, knowing that your grandkids and all the kids in your neighborhood can read well and excel in school and in life.

Imagine how proud you will be when schools across this state turn out kids who are taught to read and think critically, ready for college, ready for a career, ready for the challenges and opportunities of life in the twenty-first century.

Imagine how proud you will be when America once again has the best and brightest students because they can read and learn—and our country will not be listed more than halfway down the pack of developed countries in literacy and math.

You don't have to imagine; you can make it happen.

It is no secret that reading is the foundation for all of education, without which there is no education. New literacy law can fix this. Science has proven that we can teach all students to read; we know how, but we don't do it because we don't have to. Reading can make the difference between going to college and going to jail.

Just a few hours of your time can make a difference. Go to our website and sign up. Join the effort to ensure that all children learn to read.

We can't be silent and sit on the sidelines while this crisis threatens to take down our country. If you don't help, who will?

Will you join us?

CHAPTER SEVEN
MY PERSONAL REFLECTIONS

> *"There are risks and costs to a program of action. But they are far less than the long-range risks and costs of comfortable inaction."*
>
> —John F. Kennedy

I have come to realize that comfortable inaction is no longer an option, for me or for any of us, really. If we want to see our children and grandchildren thrive, if we want to see America remain supreme as the world's leader of human rights, prosperity, great ideals, and achievements, we must face the tremendous challenge of instituting reading literacy as a mandate for American students. The more quickly we work together as a cohesive community with a shared vision and commitment, the more quickly we will triumph in our goal for a booming, literate nation. As so well articulated by Rinku Sen, author of *Stir*

It Up, "Organizing is essentially the process of creating politically active constituencies out of people with problems by focusing on the strengths and the solutions embedded in their experience." Accordingly, we can rally to make great things happen in America. Or, you and I can remain resigned to the present condition of failing millions of our young that stand no chance of becoming successful people. It is our choice to choose or not to choose reading literacy legislation. And, in our choice, we either fail the future of our great country or we harness our will and create a literate nation. There are no options in between.

Let me make it clear that I have never really been an activist. I have worked hard and met life's challenges. I grew up in the old America that demanded I become a college-educated citizen and participate fully in society. Try as I might to stay in my old, contented world with my blinders focused on "my" future; try as I might to let others "who know more" handle the challenges in America; try as I might, I am no longer comfortable. No longer can I ignore, pretend, or escape from the fact that U.S. education is adversely affecting America's social, political, and economic health. Nor can I overlook the psychological damage U.S. education is doing to tens of millions of individuals who cannot participate in modern society's demand for lifelong learning. So, out of fear rather than desire, I must wear the term "education-activists."

My journeys lead me to witness a state of education emergency that commands we fix the problems. Both on a large scale and as individuals and volunteers on a small scale, addressing the imperative of literacy for the vitality of our nation is mandated, *now.* For twenty years we have failed to seriously tackle an education system that has worsened in time and can no longer be ignored. You, too, are aware that we live in a world that eliminates old jobs, faster and faster, and is ever more complex and demanding—a world that requires more from each of us. When my forty-year-old stepson (who soared during the dot-com boom and recently, as an entrepreneur sold his company to a leading multinational firm) said, "I am having a hard time keeping up with changes in new media," my heart missed a beat. Here we have an extremely literate, Ivy League alumnus admitting he is "challenged" to keep up. At that moment, I was upset not for my stepson, but rather for the millions of students that U.S. education is failing to give even the most basic skill required to prosper on today's complex world stage—reading literacy—much less an Ivy League education.

In the process of this journey, I continue to reflect on my life stories that have led me to this point of action. I played an active role in both of my children's education because of their learning challenges. My daughter, who just turned thirty and propelled herself in short order to become the managing director of a leading, multinational advertising firm, struggled with learning to read and write. Because she is gifted, she also managed to hide it very well. Her beautiful private school that sits on top of a hill in San Francisco continued to tell me she was bright and that reading was a "maturation issue" for her. "It will come in time," her teachers and the head mistress repeatedly told me, as both my daughter and I struggled through the pains of nightly homework and aching tears. It was not until she reached the fifth grade that I stopped believing her teachers and took action. Her tender self-esteem had suffered, and my guilt about my ignorance mounted into a self-directed anger. How could I have trusted "them" with my precious daughter's future? How could I have been so stupid?

For my daughter, there is an amazing ending. Thankfully, we found a highly skilled, expert education therapist along with a new school that guided her to become reading literate. She worked so hard to catch up, and honestly it took a village and a small fortune, but college proved fruitful as she soared, achieving honors followed by frequent promotions in business. But, in retrospect, what is most disappointing is how her heart broke in those early years, how mine did, too, and how it could have been circumvented if her kindergarten or first-grade teachers had been properly instructed in the complexities of reading development and assessments. If they had, my daughter would have achieved reading literacy before beginning the fourth grade.

Then, there is my son's story, which also compels me to stay the course and do all I can for kids, parents, and teachers. I will never forget "our" moment in time—a moment I could kick myself for again and again. A moment that should have been prevented because all the warning signs were there and I missed them, again, just as I had with my daughter. The forewarning was similar but different enough that they did not catch my attention. Regardless, I had no excuse; the school had no excuse. However, the teachers had an excuse and it was called ignorance—ignorance in understanding at-risk readers. Yes, pure ignorance was why my son had been held back in kindergarten for "extra time to mature," and why I will never forget that very moment I realized that he was *seriously* struggling with the second grade.

In my most profound reflection I recall that autumn evening, on my knees lovingly helping my son from his warm shower. As I looked into his beautiful eyes, they were tearful and oh, so filled with despair. His small, second-grade hands gripped my shoulders tightly. I asked him what was wrong. And, with heartbreaking sadness and deep anguish, he gulped back his little sobs and said, "Mom, when will I be able to read the blackboard like all my friends?" This agonizing moment is etched so strongly in my mind that I still tear up at its memory, thirteen years later. It tore at my soul beyond words and continues to move me to ensure that no other mother or child will ever have to feel the grief we felt at that moment.

Like my daughter, in time my son was blessed with remarkable and highly skilled teachers of reading. Today he attends a prestigious university and will graduate this year with a degree in engineering, management, and information systems. To say the least, it is an ambitious "3D" degree, well suited for success in the twenty-first century. My son has soared through summer internships, both international and national, and has already been offered a position after graduation. For this, I am proud and grateful. However, had we not found qualified teachers and schools, just as easily both my son and daughter could have dropped out of high school, unable to read their textbooks or pass their exams, unable to write coherently, and thoroughly unprepared to think critically and prosper in this complex world.

Another story that keeps me on this journey for student literacy is a nameless, loving grandmother who once touched my arm and said to me, "I don't want my grandchild to be stupid because he can't read." As with my children's struggles, neither will this moment leave me—her earnest face, her caring, sad eyes, her emotional request for my help, and my utter feeling of helplessness. I was so ignorant about education that I didn't know how to guide her then, for we were in sisterhood, searching to help our families. With hindsight, there is so much I could have done; I just didn't think I had the tools to do anything. To this very day, I wonder about her pain and what happened to her grandson.

"Don't be too timid and squeamish about your actions. All life is an experiment."

—Ralph Waldo Emerson

I hope these heartfelt reflections clarify my quest to act on behalf of all children and America's future. I cannot rest, I can only dream and carefully choreograph my long days to help education.

After much struggle and heartbreak, I am doubly blessed that both of my SEEDS children have flourished. This should be the right of all our nation's people. I am so grateful to read every day of my life, for I understand that literacy is my gateway to independent lifetime learning and decision making, to critical thinking about an ever-changing world, and to participation in the explosion of new media. I want this for all Americans—the ability to fully partake in society.

Relentlessly, my travels through the country and the world awaken me to the ubiquitous erosion of U.S. education. Like all of us, I earnestly want the continuation of America's great democracy, innovation, culture, and arts. Like all of us, I understand that with an uneducated populace, America could fall from ascendancy and possibly mislay democracy. Thus, for my children and grandchildren, as well as yours, I am frightened into action, committed to change the fact that our students are getting lost in the literacy abyss.

Plain, simple, and possible: America must take up the challenges of literacy and education in almost every state in this country. This will require that we invest in transformation: "ReTrain, ReDesign and ReBuild" our teachers, school methodology and education's workforce. Why? The future of our children and our great country demands it. As so well summarized by Michael Gecan in his book *Going Public*, "So leaders and organizers face a tough challenge... We are called to love, engage, and uphold our most cherished institutions, while watching them, questioning them, and pressing upon them to change, all at the same time."

Ultimately, we cannot decree change by talking and writing knowledgeable papers; rather, we must press upon ourselves and our institutions to face the tough challenges, to become leaders of transformation, to look to science for direction, and to step up to the plate of action. Our power must come in the "doing," moving forward, sharing our unflinching conviction, and seizing the power to act for America's future.

— Cinthia Coletti Haan

CHAPTER EIGHT

"There's just three things I'd ever say:
If anything goes bad, I did it.
If anything goes semi-good, then we did it.
If anything goes real good, then you did it.
That's all it takes to get people to win foot-
ball games for you."

— Paul (Bear) Bryant

Summary: The U.S. Literacy Deficit Commands State Literacy Law

It has been such a pleasure to work on the model legislation, which I am about to present in summary. In collaboration with teachers, education therapists, scientists, school administrators, and experts around the country, we have taken the time to examine and write logical, dynamic, and ready-to-implement "science-proven and practice-based legislation." It is now time to walk the walk rather than talk the talk.

Visit www.state-literacy-law.org for the complete body of work. It is designed to equip your school's leaders, principals and reading teacher so your students become reading literate, college/career ready, lifelong learners. Furthermore, it will help schools realize the value of Common Core State Standards designed to propel young people to partake in all that society offers. In turn, the nation will begin its journey back to the top of international educational standings.

As I speak to folks around the country who are working with their legislators to enact law, I am in awe and full of respect for their dedication to the greater good. They are out there every day working for kids and for our country—they are educating, mending philosophical bridges, helping teachers and schools in their practices, and mostly, they are helping students attain reading literacy through policy. I am fully empowered by *their* power.

Tomorrow I will meet with our San Francisco School District superintendent, Carlos Garcia. Together we are seeking ways to train hundreds of PK–12 teachers in the all components recommended in the Literacy Law. I can't imagine doing this a year ago; but now I am confident in the body of work and the science that supports it. It is time to begin leadership efforts within all of our states, cities, and in my own back yard with Carlos. It is time to solicit local companies and corporations to help us fund this endeavor, now, before another child falls behind and starts the process of becoming a high school dropout. Education transformation and Literacy Law are so much easier when we have a clear, consistent framework to prepare students for college and the workforce. This is what Literacy Law can do and what the Standards can do.

It is time to begin…

"Overview" for Model State Literacy Laws, Regulatory Requirements

The prosperity of a country's citizenship is not a birthright, it is a triumph that has to be earned year after year through sound policies that unleash the natural capacities of its people. A country's greatest asset is its human capital. Human capital that must become literate and educated, both of which are the gift of freedom a country endows its future.

Literacy Law Foreword

A fundamental right in America is the right to a free, appropriate public education. Critical to the success, happiness, and freedom for each young citizen is to receive a world-class, public education, one that intellectually empowers them to accomplish their dreams. "Appropriate" public education equates to academic achievement that leads to college and/or career readiness and encourages the individual to start the journey down the road to choice and freedom. The largest barrier to student educational achievement is failure to become literate—the ability to read with understanding, to write coherently, to think critically about printed material, and to reflect on information. Literacy failure is most often associated with poor classroom reading instruction, poverty, limited English proficiency, learning disabilities, and dyslexia. Only 33 percent of U.S. fourth-grade students scored as proficient, grade-level readers on the nation's report card, NAEP. This means that nearly seven in ten students are not achieving grade-level reading literacy. Of these seven students, just over half (55 percent) are *not* poor, meaning they are not eligible for free or reduced price school lunch, but rather from middle- and upper-class families. Extensive research funded through the National Institutes of Health and other agencies shows that the vast majority of student literacy failure is unnecessary; essentially, reading failure can be prevented or ameliorated through good reading instruction.

In the U.S. and elsewhere in the world, scholars have found a direct correlation between levels of literacy, wealth, poverty, and the general quality of life. All students have the potential to make important and unique contributions to society, as evidenced by millions of successful entrepreneurs, innovators, business people, cultural and community leaders, teachers, scholars, engineers, and others who have overcome obstacles and become reading literate. Conversely, today in our schools, millions of at-risk students are not being served well by public education and, thus, are unable to reach their potential. Some of the poorest citizens are functionally illiterate, living in urban ghettos and rural communities where high school diplomas and college degrees are in short supply. Almost all of these people at one time were students who clearly were not given proper reading instruction and were shuffled through the system ill prepared for self-sustaining citizenship and its freedoms. Functional illiteracy leaves young people powerless to create a viable identity, of which the consequences are widely understood: frustration, anger, school dropout, crime, drugs, underemployment, and social dependency. This is an injustice. Not teaching our young people proficient reading literacy to achieve an education, maintain self-esteem, and have the freedom to support themselves makes them victims and relegates them to the bottom of society—young people with no skills, education, values, or aspirations.

The documented costs of these social consequences represent extraordinary hardships, both financially and morally, to our nation, each state, and every community. Scholars and history highlight that an uneducated population generates welfare entitlements that, over time, fuel resentment and cause governmental disruption. On the other hand, a significant but far smaller investment in rigorous literacy training of all teachers of reading, effective classroom reading instruction, early at-risk student identification through screening and assessment, and appropriate classroom support services for at-risk students will ensure a more fulfilled, educated, and productive citizenry. Making this investment will boost the overall growth of every community, region, workforce, business, civic group, and religious group as well as gross state product and the nation's gross domestic product. If we wish to remain a free and productive nation, it is compulsory for the citizens of every state to create generations of educated young people, prepared to tackle, fulfill, innovate, contribute, and form twenty-first-century communities, governments, and workforces.

Literacy Law Rationale

Literacy Law is imperative to ensure all students are reading literate as appropriate for their grade level. The goal of the Literacy Law is for all students to graduate from high school fully prepared to participate in modern society as individuals capable of contributing to their own success and that of their communities, workforce, and governments. Therefore, it is crucial that all students achieve proficient reading and literacy skills needed to be lifelong learners.

The Literacy Law is also a directive to realize the Common Core State Standards (Standards) for students' education. As with the Literacy Law, the Standards were developed in collaboration with teachers, school administrators, and experts to provide a clear and consistent framework to prepare students for college and the workforce. For Literacy Law and the Standards to be realized, it is incumbent upon the districts and schools within each state to ensure all students achieve reading literacy. Reading literacy moves from the classroom to the workplace, to citizenship, to lifelong learning, which is central to achieving individual aspirations.

The Literacy Law and the Standards, which are informed by science and the most effective models from states across the country and countries around the world, give teachers and parents a common understanding of what students are expected to learn. Consistent state Literacy Law and Standards provide appropriate benchmarks for all students, regardless of where they live or the school they attend.

The Literacy Law defines the knowledge and skills that three levels of *teachers* must master: (1) *teachers of reading* in grades K–3, (2) *teaching specialists* in reading, ELL, Title I, and special education in grades K–12, and (3) *content areas teachers* in grades 4–12. The Standards define the knowledge and skills that *students* must master within their K–12 education careers. Both the Literacy Law and the Standards share the goal that students will graduate high school able to succeed in entry-level, credit-bearing academic college courses and in workforce training programs.

The Literacy Law and the Standards:

1. Are aligned with college and work expectations
2. Are clear, understandable, and consistent
3. Include rigorous content and application of knowledge through high-order skills
4. Build upon strengths and lessons of current state standards
5. Are informed by other top-performing countries, so that all students are prepared to succeed in our global economy and society
6. Are data-validated/evidence-based

For the Literacy Law and the Standards to be achieved, every district, school, and teacher must ensure that all students meet or exceed grade-level reading proficiency (reading literacy) in all content subjects, such as science, math, technology, and English

Language Arts. To accomplish this directive, both the Literacy Law and the Standards have directives for reading literacy development in the following areas:

> Reading Foundational Skills are directed toward fostering students' understanding and working knowledge of concepts of print, the alphabetic principle, and other basic conventions of the English writing system. These foundational skills are not an end in and of themselves; rather, they are necessary and important components of an effective, comprehensive core reading and language program designed to develop proficient readers with the capacity to comprehend texts across a range of types and disciplines. Instruction should be differentiated: good readers will need much less practice with these concepts than SEEDS will. A Multitier System of Supports will be integrated into general education instruction. The point is to teach students what they need to learn and not what they already know—to discern when particular children or activities warrant more or less attention.
>
> Reading Literacy Skills offer a focus for instruction each year and help ensure that students gain adequate exposure to a range of texts and tasks. Rigor is also infused through the requirement that students read increasingly complex texts through the grades. Thus, grade-level reading proficiency is required for each grade. Students advancing through the grades are expected to meet each year's grade-specific standards and retain or further develop skills and understandings mastered in preceding grades.
>
> Writing Skills offer a focus for instruction each year to help ensure that students gain adequate mastery of a range of skills and applications. Each year in their writing, students should demonstrate increasing sophistication in all aspects of language use, from vocabulary and syntax to the development and organization of ideas, and they should address increasingly

demanding content and sources. Students advancing through the grades are expected to meet each year's grade-specific standards and retain or further develop skills and understandings mastered in preceding grades.

Speaking, Listening, and Language Skills offer a focus for instruction each year to help ensure that students gain adequate mastery of a range of skills and applications. Students advancing through the grades are expected to meet each year's grade-specific standards and retain or further develop skills and understandings mastered in preceding grades.

Literacy Law Component Summary

1. Standards and Certification for Teachers of Reading, Teaching Specialists, and Content Area Teachers

The Literacy Law and the Standards are determined by ongoing clinical research that concludes reading teachers use knowledge and skills provided in their teacher preparation and professional development programs to either *help* **or** *hinder* a class of diverse students learning to develop reading skills. It has been proven that data-validated, comprehensive teacher preparation and professional development programs produce "expert" teachers of reading who are qualified to ensure the students, for which they are responsible, thrive and become reading literate. When teacher preparation programs and professional development programs leave out essential data-validated reading instruction methods and knowledge, teachers are not adequately prepared to teach reading in a way that will positively affect all students, especially SEEDS, achieve grade-level reading. We must remember that a shocking 67 percent of students (NAEP) are reading *below* proficiency. Without grade-level reading proficiency, the Standards cannot be achieved. Therefore, this law commences a requirement for the certification for all professionals who teach reading in the state to pass the ***Advanced*** *Reading Instruction Competence Assessment* and become a Certified Teacher of Reading, and that all "content area teachers" pass the *Basic Reading Instruction Competence Assessment.*

To achieve the goals of the Literacy Law and the Standards, key professionals and candidates in the field of education, especially those responsible for teaching reading and English Language Arts, need and deserve the highest quality instruction, support, and the most data-validated training possible to achieve a certificate to become a professional teacher of reading. University and college preparation programs and ongoing professional development programs must provide data-validated knowledge, skills, and support for success.

The Literacy Law hereby defines specific requirements for three levels of teachers: (1) teachers of reading in grades K–3, (2) teaching specialists in reading, ELL, Title I, and special education in grades K–12, and (3) content area teachers in grades K–12. These teachers are required to achieve appropriate knowledge and skills in reading literacy and to pass a Reading Instruction Competence Assessment:

Teachers of Reading will be certified by the state and hereby defined as highly skilled experts in reading literacy, qualified educational professionals who have passed the *Advanced Reading Instruction Competence Assessment* and are permitted to teach reading to all children in grades K–3.

Teaching Specialists will achieve a Certificate as a "Teacher of Reading" along with the specialty licensure in reading, English Language Learners, Title I, and Special Education in grades K–12. Teaching specialists must pass the *Advanced Reading Instruction Competence Assessment* to become certified. The *Advanced Reading Instruction Competence Assessment* ensures that these teachers are highly skilled and knowledgeable in the following areas of content knowledge: foundations of reading development, development of reading comprehension, reading assessment and instruction, and integration of knowledge and understanding for reading literacy, writing, speaking, listening, and language skills.

Content Area Teachers are teachers of subjects who will take exams to be receive content area licensure and are required to pass the

Basic Reading Instruction Assessment, covering basic knowledge of the foundations of reading development, development of reading comprehension, reading instruction and assessment, and integration of knowledge and understanding so their students can become literate in their content areas: math, science, social studies, etc.

By virtue of passing the Assessment and being awarded the certificate, these teachers will be deeply respected and honored as true professionals, able to use their knowledge, expertise, and evolving experience in dynamic and flexible ways during daily interactions with diverse student populations, ensuring that all students become reading literate and life-long learners.

The Literacy Law and Standards require both higher education and school cultures to recognize that every teacher is a reading teacher, because reading is involved in every subject area. Therefore, reading strategies will be implemented in all teacher preparation programs, in professional development, and as a school-wide program in connection with a school culture and vision that work toward high levels of student achievement in reading literacy. All requirements of the Literacy Law and Standards highlight that all teachers and schools will provide every opportunity for students to read and practice their strategies, in every subject, every day, to enhance their development of the reading skills they need to become better readers and, ultimately, reading literate.

2. Screening, Formal Assessment, and Gathering Data

The Literacy Law and the Standards set forth that student success is achieved through a sustainable system of supports and strategies that are constructed to deliver continuous assessment, evaluation, and communication of students' reading progress. In many schools and districts, student data analysis has not been viewed as a high priority. To achieve the Common Core State Standards, the Literacy Law mandates that great emphasis be given to both school and student data to analyze teacher, program, and system effectiveness. Data will be gathered to guide students' reading literacy and educational success by requiring that all districts, schools, and education staff become familiar with data analysis: (1) collecting and interpreting both school and student data; (2) sharing data; (3) framing questions from analysis of multiple sets of data reports; and (4) creating plans to assist individual student achievement.

The Literacy Law furthers requires that each district and school will: (1) establish a school-wide data use plan and ongoing review of plan implementation to monitor student progress toward goals; (2) guide and support teachers in use of data for instructional improvement to meet the needs of students and to support students in reaching their goals; (3) support and lead both students and their parents to be on track for postsecondary success by selecting goals and monitoring their progress toward those goals; and (4) ensure that school-level and student data needs are incorporated in district-wide data management systems planning and implementation.

The Literacy Law requires that data be continuously utilized to provide new insights into student learning and how to improve it. This process is implemented so that schools and teachers can replace hunches and hypotheses with facts by utilizing data to identify the root causes of student learning problems, not just the symptoms. With data, all districts, schools, and teachers will collect, analyze, and require: (1) clear assessment on students' needs; (2) the expertise to target resources to address students' needs; (3) the ability to set student goals; (4) the aptitude to determine whether the goals are being reached; and (5) the ability to track the impact of staff development efforts.

The Literacy Law further requires the application of a data use plan under which students, PK–12, enrolled or enrolling in public schools, are screened and assessed for literacy failure/grade-level reading attainment as may be necessary and that they be provided appropriate supports dependent on multiple factors and at multiple times until proficient grade-level reading skills are secured.

3. General Education Classroom Core Reading and Language Instruction for All Students

The Literacy Law set forth that to achieve the Standards, the most powerful foundation that can be provided to all students is reading literacy, for it is the first stepping stone toward educational and lifelong learning accomplishments. Put simply, reading literacy affords students the opportunity to flourish and participate in society, capable of reflective thinking. Reading literacy is best accomplished by first developing a progression of language skills that, in time, lead to a deep understanding and the intellectual process of gaining meaning from printed material.

The Literacy Law requires that all core reading and language instruction programs be data --validated/evidence based and consist of the Standards: Reading Foundational Skills; Reading Literacy Skills; Writing Skills; and Speaking, Listening, and Language Skills. It is understood that reading literacy is attained through a complex development progression best taught by highly skilled and well-trained professional teachers of reading, who have mastered reading and language instruction and the Multitier System of Supports in teaching to a diverse student population.

The Literacy Law requires core reading and language classroom reading instruction in grades K–3 to include components in: (1) Language-Based Instruction that integrates all aspects of language to include receptive and expressive language, written expression, and handwriting; (2) Phonological Awareness; (3) Phoneme-Grapheme Correspondence Knowledge; (4) Syllable Instruction; (5) Linguistics; (6) Meaning-Based Instruction; (7) Reading Fluency Instruction; and (8) Phonics.

4. Multitier System of Supports for Reading Literacy Attainment

The Literacy Law requires that students be identified early for reading failure through screenings and assessments. This is imperative for the Standards to be achieved. The Multitier System Supports (MTSS) is designed to screen, assess, and provide general education tiers of instruction and intervention to individual students who struggle with differing aspects of learning to become reading proficient. MTSS is designed for teachers of reading to scaffold instruction for SEEDS in small class settings at the first signs of falling behind lesson accomplishment. The major instructional strategies of MTSS utilize individualized data to determine intensive and multi-component methods as appropriate for the reading, writing, and spelling proficiency of each student. Extensive research and numerous syntheses have been conducted in the area of reading instruction and intervention for reading difficulties to be ameliorated and/or eradicated. In particular, the Institute for Education Sciences has issued a guidance document to help schools improve instruction for SEEDS.

The Literacy Law and Standards require that teachers and schools no longer wait until a student is significantly behind grade-level reading before assessing skills and providing supports. Each school will provide continual, data-driven assessment on each student and provide MTSS intervention quickly and as needed for each student's reading literacy attainment. [Note: MTSS is also known as Response to Intervention (RTI).]

The Literacy Law set forth that once in force, students currently in grades PK–3 will achieve grade-level reading proficiency by fourth grade. However, for SEEDS who have missed the opportunity to become reading literate by grades 4–12, all schools will provide reading interventions that serve as an alternative to English Language Arts class. The Literacy Law and Standards require a school culture that recognizes that every content area teacher is a reading teacher, because reading is involved in every subject area. Therefore, reading strategies will be implemented as a school-wide program in connection with a school culture and vision that work toward high levels of student achievement in reading literacy. Specific interventions and strategies will be provided to support SEEDS who have struggled to learn to read in early elementary school and are currently performing below grade level in reading. All schools will provide every opportunity for students to read and practice their strategies in every subject, every day, to enhance their development of the reading skills they need to become better readers and, ultimately, reading literate.

5. Responsibilities of School Districts to Enact the Literacy Law and Standards

Both the Literacy Law and the Standards require each district, school, and charter school to comply with all procedures outlined to ensure each student's academic success and career/college readiness. Every school system has specific responsibilities for implementation of the law. They are as follows: (1) create and adopt school system policies and procedures for implementation of the law; (2) guarantee ongoing, clear public notification regarding the school's and the district's obligations toward assurance of certified teachers of reading, reading specialists, and content area teachers; (3) provide training and professional development in reading literacy for content area teachers to pass the Basic Reading Instruction Competence Assessment; (4) provide informal training and professional development in reading literacy for system representatives, teachers, paraprofessionals, appropriate staff, and administrators on an annual basis; (5) ensure that each school within the system selects personnel to oversee the assessment process for determination of program success with the Literacy Law and the Standards; (6) ensure that MTSS programs for students with SEEDS meet the state criteria and follow the appropriate guidelines to include formal diagnostic assessment of students; and (7) ensure that each school within the system follows regulations for implementation of the law by providing for the functional and academic needs of students identified as below proficient in grade-level reading.

6. Guidelines and Standards for Implementation of the Literacy Law

While the converging evidence from research conducted over several decades has provided a great deal of knowledge related to what is needed to improve literacy and education outcomes for all students, little attention has been paid to *how* states, districts, and schools will put practices into place that will indeed meet the learning needs of all students and SEEDS. More recent research studies examining the implementation of social programs around the globe have provided a framework for implementing systems change to achieve better outcomes from investments in such programs. Even the most significantly evidence-based/data-validated core reading and language programs and MTSS interventions will not make a difference for children if teachers do not implement them or implement them ineffectively. "Since sound and effective implementation requires change at the practice, organization, and systems level, processes must be purposeful to create change in the knowledge, behavior, and attitudes of all the human service professionals and partners involved" (Blasé, Van Dyke, & Fixsen, 2010). Given what we know from research, this law requires states, districts, and schools to utilize the findings for *what* we need to do to improve learning outcomes and *how* to do it.

The Literacy Law and Standards require funding to build an implementation infrastructure to ensure appropriate and sufficient resources are made available to build state and local capacity to meet the requirements of this law. The Literacy Law, along with a state plan for capacity-building, will be readily available to the public through the website of the state board of education, in print and available through an interpreter.

Literacy Law Definitions

Literacy
Literacy represents the lifelong, intellectual process of gaining meaning from print. Key to all literacy is reading development, which involves a progression of skills that begins with the ability to understand spoken words and decode written words and culminates in the deep understanding of text. Reading development involves

a range of complex language underpinnings including awareness of speech sounds (phonology), spelling patterns (orthography), word meaning (semantics), grammar (syntax), and patterns of word formation (morphology), all of which provide a necessary platform for reading fluency and comprehension. Once these skills are acquired, the reader can attain full English literacy, which includes the abilities to approach printed material with critical analysis, inference, and synthesis; to write with accuracy and coherence; and to use information and insights from text as the basis for informed decisions and creative thought.

Literacy Failure

Literacy Failure represents the entire spectrum of reading difficulties that, if not eradicated, may be experienced from childhood to adulthood. In the U.S., approximately seven out of ten students in fourth grade and eighth grade (67 percent) fail to read proficiently enough to comprehend text-level reading (National Assessment of Educational Progress), and scholars report that this deficiency characteristically continues through adulthood. As this reading gap widens into secondary school, it is likely to result in increased high school dropout rates. Understanding and addressing the sources of literacy failure will ensure that this large portion of the student population is met with correct instruction and support systems to ensure academic achievement and life skills.

Reading Literacy

Reading Literacy is a term that has evolved over time with changes in society, the economy, and cultures. According to the Organisation for Economic Co-operation and Development (OECD), reading literacy goes beyond reading's required development of active and interactive skill attainment and beyond comprehension of rich text. Reading literacy implies there is a capacity for reflection on written material that initiates personal experiences and memories as well as cognitive function. Reading literacy moves from the classroom to the workplace, to citizenship, to life-long learning, which is central to achieving individual aspirations. Reading literacy also affords the reader a set of linguistic tools that are increasingly important for meeting the requests of modern society, from interaction with peers and communities to interactions with large bureaucracies and complex legal systems. To attain reading literacy, a student must be taught to first utilize a wide range of reading and literacy skills that will develop into subject matter literacy, such as science literacy or math literacy. Reading literacy is the building block to understanding all subject matter. Reading literacy unleashes the potential to enrich and extend one's personal life and empowers one to participate fully in society.

SEEDS

SEEDS is the acronym for students who are at risk of failing to attain proficient, grade-level reading and literacy abilities. SEEDS are comprised of a variety of groups: Struggling readers, Economically disadvantaged youth, English language learners, students with Dyslexia, and Specific Learning Disability students. SEEDS have diverse needs that make early reading development to grade-level reading literacy problematic for numerous reasons (see individual definitions below). All SEEDS can be recognized early and given instruction appropriate to their needs. Research has shown that the largest barrier to SEEDS attaining academic success is the failure to receive proper reading instruction and supports. This missed opportunity prevents SEEDS from becoming grade-level learners and thus reduces their opportunity to secure a secondary degree or post-secondary degree or to be equipped with the skills needed for twenty-first-century employment. If appropriate instruction supports are provided, SEEDS will maintain their self-esteem and flourish, becoming proficient at reading literacy with the ability to understand text, to write accurately and coherently, to think critically about subject matter, and to reflect on the world around them. [It is important to note that SEEDS categories are not exclusive; for example, SEEDS may be English language learners and also dyslexia students.]

Struggling Readers

Struggling Readers have difficulty developing reading skills for numerous reasons, almost all of which can be eradicated through early identification, systematic assessment, analysis, and appropriate instruction. Whether instructional, environmental, cultural, genetic, or developmental in nature, all sub-standard readers need to be identified early, in pre-K–Kindergarten preferably. They also need to be engaged in science-based, core reading and language instruction, assessed systematically, and given a system of supports toward the goal of reading proficiency by third grade. Struggling readers in grades 4–12 will require interventions that serve as an alternative to English Language Arts class. Teachers of reading will teach reading skills and comprehensive reading supports with intensity and through assessable texts in content subject areas.

A sub-group of struggling readers may be diverse learners who have difficulty learning to read because of certain mild limitations in cognition and communication, but they can be taught to read by utilizing their strengths. Diverse learners often need the support of technologies and strategies to develop skills in reading literacy in general education classes. Any student characterized by difficulties or differences in learning academic skills, that are not consistent with the person's chronological age, intellectual capacity, or educational opportunities, and that cannot be explained by the presence of an intellectual disability, sensory disorder, or emotional disorder, may be termed a struggling reader, diverse learner.

Economically Disadvantaged Youth

Economically Disadvantaged Youth often enter school significantly behind and less prepared than their more well-to-do peers. Their academic disadvantage is seen in everything from impoverished language input in early childhood (letter awareness and spoken vocabulary) to number awareness and self-control. By mid-second grade, these students often are even further behind their peers in language skills as a result of poor quality or inappropriate reading instruction. Students in this category will require diverse systems of support appropriate to their literacy needs beginning in pre-K through third grade. Many of these students are "Title I Eligible" and receive "Free and/or Reduced Lunch," meaning the federal Elementary and Secondary Act provide financial assistance to local educational agencies and schools with high numbers or high percentages of children from low-income families to help ensure that all children meet challenging state academic standards.

English Language Learners and/or Students with Limited English Proficiency

English Language Learners (ELL) and/or Students with Limited English Proficiency (LEP) have recently come to the U.S. from another country, have parents who speak a foreign language at home, or are older students of poor instruction, often as a result of cultural-linguistic perception differences. ELL and LEP students are becoming the majority minority in many public schools. With more immigrants having arrived in the U.S. during the 1990s than in any other decade, the number of public school students needing additional language instruction has increased dramatically in recent years (Bureau of U.S. Citizenship and Immigration Services, 2001). A survey of state education agencies found that, in 2004, more than 5.5 million students with limited proficiency in English were enrolled in public schools across the nation, making up almost 10 percent of the total kindergarten-twelfth-grade public school enrollment. The population of students who are ELL has grown 105 percent, while the general school population has grown only 12 percent since the 1990-91 school year. States report more than 460 languages spoken by students with limited proficiency in English (Kindler, 2002), with 80 percent of the students speaking Spanish. These burgeoning numbers pose unique challenges for educators striving to ensure that language-minority students achieve to high levels.

Achievement data suggest that students with LEP lag far behind their peers. Nationwide, only 7 percent of these students scored "at or above proficient" in reading on the National Assessment of Educational Progress, compared to about 33 percent of students overall. Results in fourth-grade math, as well as eighth-grade reading and math, were similar. Findings support that limited verbal language proficiency does not constrain a student's emergent reading and writing development. Limited English language students are capable of making sense of written input while they are working on becoming fluent speakers of English (Fitzgerald & Noblit, 1999; Weber & Longhi-Chirlin, 1996). This research orientation maintains that just as speaking, reading, and writing are interrelated in the emerging literacy of native speakers, they are equally related in the emerging literacy of second-language students.

Dyslexia

Dyslexia, neurobiological in origin, is characterized by difficulties with accurate and/or fluent word recognition and by poor spelling and decoding abilities. These difficulties typically result from a deficit in the phonological component of language, which is often unexpected in relation to other cognitive abilities and the provision of effective classroom instruction. Secondary consequences may include problems in reading comprehension and reduced reading experience that can impede the growth of vocabulary and background knowledge (National Institutes of Child Health and Human Development and the International Dyslexia Association).

Dyslexia is usually characterized by early difficulties with accurate and/or fluent word recognition and poor spelling, and later by difficulties with text-level fluency, leading to problems with written comprehension and sometimes writing. Students with dyslexia represent a continuum of underlying difficulties, typically beginning with weaknesses in the phonological component of language and in the speed of processing multiple, language-related components of reading. These difficulties can be found singly or, more typically, together. Importantly, they are largely unexpected in relation to other, often-strong cognitive abilities in the student and the provision of otherwise effective instruction. Some students who have both decoding and fluency issues and who receive effective decoding instruction go on to have only fluency-based issues that affect comprehension and the quality and quantity of their reading. Whatever the pathway, reduced reading can impede the growth of all language capacities, particularly vocabulary and grammar, which then can impede the development of background knowledge necessary for advances in learning. Further dyslexia characteristics are often witnessed in rote math calculations and in speech, specifically word retrieval and processing speed. Appropriate interventions can change the course of these students' academic careers.

Dyslexia and Specific Learning Disabilities represent approximately one third of all literacy failure groups and may require intensive, appropriately matched intervention as early as possible. Kindergarten screening most often will identify these students early, so core reading instruction and systems of support can lead to good reading skills through life.

Specific Learning Disability

Specific Learning Disability, as defined by the Individuals with Disabilities Education Act of 2004, is a disorder in one or more of the basic psychological processes involved in understanding or using language, spoken or written, that may manifest itself in the imperfect ability to listen, think, speak, read, write, spell, or do mathematical calculations, including conditions such as perceptual disabilities, brain injury, minimal brain dysfunction, dyslexia, and developmental aphasia. Specific Learning Disability does not include learning problems or intellectual disabilities that create limitations in mental functioning that are mostly dealt with in special education environments and are primarily the result of visual, hearing, or motor disabilities; mental retardation; or emotional disturbance.

Specific Learning Disabilities can include meta-cognitive strategy development and self-regulation (Fletcher, Lyon, Fuchs, Barnes,

& Vaughn, 2010) such as those with attention deficit and hyperactivity disorders and those with dysgraphia (Berninger, 2004), both of whom display written expression problems. Research provides six clear classifications of learning disabilities: 1) word reading (dyslexia), 2) reading fluency, 3) reading comprehension, 4) written expression, 5) mathematics calculation (dyscalculia), and 6) mathematics problem solving. Each of these disabilities has a distinct cognitive correlate for which there is specific evidence-based intervention.

Teachers of Reading and Teaching Specialists
Teachers of Reading are defined as educational professionals who teach classroom reading instruction to all students in grades pre-K through third grade. Certified teachers of reading have passed the *Advanced Reading Instruction Competence Assessment*. Teachers of reading are masters of foundation knowledge from reading development through reading literacy. **Teaching Specialists** are teachers in elementary, middle, and high school who specialize in reading instruction, English language learners instruction, Title I student instruction, and special education instruction. Reading specialists are also certified as teachers of reading who have passed the *Advanced Reading Instruction Competence Assessment*. Teachers with a certificate are considered to be highly important within a school because they teach the foundational skill necessary for all educational attainment. Passing the *Advanced Reading Instruction Competence Assessment* requires a solid knowledge base of skilled expertise in all aspects of reading instruction, data analysis and interpretation, screening, assessments, strategies, Multitier System Supports, and interventions for all students to achieve grade-level reading literacy.

A complete copy of the entire Literacy Law,
supporting documents, Common Core State Standards Initiative,
and the tools for building grassroots are available at
www.state-literacy-law.org

LITERACY LAW TEAM COLLABORATION

List of Contributors

Government Affairs Committee Chair: Cinthia Coletti Haan, Board of Directors and Chair, Government Affairs Committee, International Dyslexia Association; Chair, Haan Foundation for Children; President, Power4Kids Reading Initiative: Chair, Literate Nation

Government Affairs Administrator: Gianmarco Titolo, Education Analyst, Haan Foundation for Children; Student, Lyle School of Engineering, Southern Methodist University

IDA Government Affairs Committee:
Charlotte G. Andrist, Ph.D., NCSP, President, Central Ohio Branch of the International Dyslexia Association
Michelle Brownstein, Member of Chapel Hill-Carrboro City Schools Board of Education, Member of NCPTA Exceptional Children's Commission
Elsa Cardenas-Hagan, Ph.D., CALT, Director, Valley Speech Language and Learning Center
Margie B. Gillis, Ed.D., President, Literacy How, Inc., Research Affiliate, Haskins Laboratories
Bette V. Erickson, Co-founder, Minnesota MOMs On a Mission, Parent Advocate
Laura Kaloi, Policy Director, National Center for Learning Disabilities, Inc.
G. Reid Lyon, Ph.D., Associate Dean of the School of Education and Human Development at Southern Methodist University (SMU), distinguished professor in the Department of Education Policy and Leadership at SMU, and distinguished scientist,

Department of Cognition and Neuroscience at the Center for Brain Health, University of Texas, Dallas

Vicki Myers, Ph.D., Special Assistant to the Director, Office of Special Education, U.S. Department of Education

Stephen M. Peregoy, Executive Director, International Dyslexia Association

Scott Douglas Redmond, Venture Solutionist and Start-up Specialist, Silicon Valley

Elenn Steinberg, President, International Dyslexia Association, Rocky Mountain Branch

Cheryl Ward MS, CALP, Co-founder Literate Nation and President, Wisconsin Branch IDA

National Leaders in Education:

John Alexander, Head of School, Groves Academy

Richard Bradford, President, International Dyslexia Association, Iowa Branch

Rachel Brown-Chidsey, Ph.D., NCSP, Associate Professor of School Psychology, Co-Coordinator, SMART for Schools

Carolyn Cowen, Ed.M., Executive Director, Carroll Center for Innovative Education

Wendy Gaal, Founder, Reading Matters to Maine and literacy advisor

Stephanie M. Gordon, Northern Ohio Branch of IDA

Sally C. Grimes, Ed.M., Founding Director, The Grimes Reading Institute and Literate Nation

Pam Heyde, International Dyslexia Association, Wisconsin Branch, member of the Wisconsin Reading Coalition

Charles W. Haynes, Ed.D, CCC-SLP, Associate Professor, Department of Communication Sciences and Disorders, School of Health and Rehabilitation Sciences, MGH Institute of Health Professions

James Lanich, Executive Director, Education Results Partnership

Richard Long, Ed.D., Director, Government Relations, International Reading Association

Louisa Moats, Ed.D., President, Moats Associates Consulting, Inc. and Vice President, International Dyslexia Association

Mary Newton, J.D., Wisconsin Reading Coalition

Anthony Pedriana, Author, *Leaving Johnny Behind: Overcoming Barriers to Literacy and Reclaiming At-Risk Readers*, and former urban school teacher and principal

Caroline Sanchez Crozier, CEO/Founder, CSC Learning

Susan M. Smartt, Ph.D., Senior Research Associate, Vanderbilt University

Arlene Sonday, Fellow of the Orton-Gillingham Academy of Orton-Gillingham Practitioners and Educators

Susan Thomson, Minnesota MOMs On a Mission, Parent Advocate

Rosalie Whitlock, Ph.D., Executive Director, Children's Health Council

Maryanne Wolf, Author and Director, Center for Reading and Language Research, Eliot-Pearson Department of Child Development, Tufts University

ACKNOWLEDGMENTS

My thanks go first and foremost to my extraordinary family, Darren, Tiffany, and Giano, who support me and inspire me beyond emotion and with unconditional love. To my parents, Don and Connie, who lovingly challenge me to think first, and never settle for mediocrity. To my three archetype brothers, Marc, Jeff, and Michael, who never let me be a "wuss." To my extensive array of relatives who elevate me daily with their unconditional love and support. To my wonderful stepchildren and their children, Tommy, Michelle, Cassady, Samantha, and Kodiak, who keep me grounded in youth. And, to my irreplaceable former husbands who are and have always been my partners. And, to my Godchildren and Fairy Godchildren who bring joyfulness to my life in the most unpredicted ways.

A second round of thanks goes to my dearest friend, soul-sister, and inspiration, Maryanne Wolf, to whom I'm grateful on many levels, one being to help me find my voice in writing. To Rich Long for his encouragement to unite and end the reading divide, together. To my IDA committee members and national contributors who were at my side with input and suggestions as we focused on writing the Model State Literacy Law. To my team at The Haan Foundation for Children, the folks who fill in all the gaps and keep life seamless even when I am coming unraveled with over commitment. To my CFO and advisor, Douglas Darling, who provides trusted counsel in all aspects of my life. To my Haan Scholars, you know who you are and you have made me so very proud of you over the years. To my crazy-fun and inspiring Fairy Godsisters who deliver levity, wisdom, and therapy in equal measure: Gretchen de Baubigny, Linda Olinger, Jennifer Birch, Debbie Kovanda, Linda Howell, Sandra Gale, Diane Lyon, Jan Yanehiro, Jackie Spear, Kathryn Tunstall, Gabriella Papale, Debbi Fields, Lise Shipley, Becky de la Cruz, Linda Burton, Jan Yamagami, Margarita Panasci, and Anna Freiman.

A third round of applauses go to my esteemed and beloved colleagues who provide me with their wisdom, guidance, research, and support: Suzanne Donovan, Bruce Alberts, Kirk Clark, James Lanich, G. Reid Lyon, Peggy McCardle, Louisa Moats, Margie Gillis, Ben Shrifin, Vicki Myers, Norma Garza, Gil Noam, Joseph Torgesen, Donna Durno, Matthew Bickerton, David Myers, Greg Jones, Ben Foss, Sinclair Sherrill, Guinevere Eden, Sally Grimes, Cheryl Ward and Jim Messemer. To my early literacy instructors that provided knowledge and encouraged everlasting passion: Reid Lyon, Barbara Foreman, Dick Olson, Beth Ann Bryan, Susan Neuman, Ed Kame'enui, Doug Carnine, Sally and Bennet Shaywitz, John Gabrieli, Marcel Just, Rosalie Whitlock and Jack Fletcher. To the writers whose books I read during this process that gave me the perspectives to make this volume possible. To the Gleason Family Foundation for the momentum they helped me gain at their summer conference. And, to my editor, Claire Mullins, for all her careful attention, encouragement and hard work.

RESOURCES

Evers, W. (1998) What's Gone Wrong in America's Classrooms (pp. 49-90). Stanford, CA: Hoover Institution Press.

Luntz, F. (2010) The Language of Choice in Education. Worddoctors. com.

McCardle, P., Chhabra, V. (2004) The Voice of Evidence in Reading Research. Brooks.

Moats, L.C., (2010) Anthology of Dyslexia. IDA Press

Olshfski, D. F., Cunningham, R. B. (2008) Agendas and Decisions: How State Government Executives and Middle Managers Make and Administer Policy. State University of New York Press.

Pedriana, A. (2009) Leaving Johnny Behind. Learning Dynamics Press.

Perry, T., Moses, R., Wynne, J., Cortes, E., and Delpit, L. (2008) Quality Education as a Constitutional Right: Creating a Grassroots Movement to Transform Public Schools. Random House.

Sen, R., Klein, K. (2003) Stir It Up: Lessons in Community Organizing and Advocacy. Jossey-Bass.

Smith, S. N. (2009) Stoking the Fires of Democracy, Our Generation's Introduction to Grassroots Organizing. Pierce.

Snow, C. E., Burns, M. S., and Griffin, P. (1998) Preventing Reading Difficulties in Young Children. National Academy Press.

Stanovitch, P. J., and Stanovich, K. E. (2003) Using Research and Reason in Education: How Teachers Can Use Scientifically Based Research to Make Curricular and Instruction Decisions.

Swanson, Christopher B., Ph.D., Cities in Crisis: A Special Analytic Report on High School Graduation. EPE Research Center, and supported by America's Promise Alliance and the Bill & Melinda Gates Foundation.

Torgesen, J. K. (2002) The Prevention of Reading Difficulties. Journal School Psychology.

Wolf, M. (2007) Proust and the Squid, the Story and the Science of the Reading Brain. Washington University.

Biographies

Cinthia Coletti Haan is founder and chair of The Haan Foundation for Children, a non-profit 501(c)3 organization dedicated to uniting scientific research, education practice, and technology toward the goal of improving education for all students. She the founding partner of a new, national 501(c)(3) organization, Literate Nation, and directs the Power4Kids Reading Initiative for research in education. Ms. Coletti Haan is an advocate in Washington D.C., securing federal funding for high quality education and neuroscience research, and a national leader on state literacy and education policy reform. Through the Haan Foundation, education scholarships are provided for impoverished children requiring reading and math interventions. Haan is adamant about U.S. students receiving a world-class education to compete in the global economy. She actively supports the roles leadership, science and data play in public school transformation efforts, and advises that both student and teacher achievement data must be analyzed and used to make informed decisions that affect students' progress.

Coletti Haan facilitates a number of projects in the fields of literacy, education legislation, and neuroscience. She serves on the board of directors of several organizations, including Strategic Educational Research Partnership (SERP/National Academies of Science); California Business for Education Excellence (CBEE/EDResults); Harvard Medical School, Program in Education, Afterschool and Resiliency (PEAR); UCSF Neuroscience Initiative Leadership Council; The Department of Education Policy and Leadership at SMU; International Dyslexia Association (IDA); and SF RBI (Reviving Baseball and Literacy in Inner Cities).

Prior to dedicating her skills to science, Cinthia enjoyed more than 20 years of success in the business community, beginning as one of the founding team members in Southern Pacific Railroad's landmark launching of SPRINT, through to its acquisition by GTE. She held the position of director of Ford Aerospace, Starnet

Division, before effecting a series of mergers and acquisitions in the telecommunications industry. Coletti Haan serves as CEO of Syndacon Corporation and Coletti Investments, LLC.

Phyllis Blaunstein is senior counsel for Widmeyer Communications in Washington, D.C. She is a national leader in education policy and public engagement. She worked extensively with state boards of education to develop state policy to ensure an effective education for all children as the former executive director of the National Association of State Boards of Education, and she was an education policy fellow with the Institute for Education Leadership. Trained as a speech and language pathologist, Blaunstein directed the Speech and Hearing Clinic at the University of Tennessee Research Hospital and was a member of the faculty of the Department of Audiology and Speech Pathology at the University of Tennessee. Her work in language disorders is the precursor for her interest in providing children with research-based skills for reading.

Richard Long, Ph.D., has helped shape federal and state education policy for two decades. As director of government relations for the International Reading Association, he has worked with both the House and Senate to fashion laws such as the IDEA and the ESEA and to shepherd these laws through the rule-making process of the U.S. Department of Education. He works tirelessly for literacy, both nationally and internationally. Dr. Long is also the executive director of the National Association of State Title I Directors. He was president of the U.S. Coalition for Education for All and chaired the North American Consultation for Education for All program. Previously Dr. Long worked on the staff of Congressman James W. Symington and consulted with the U.S. Department of Education, *USA Today*, the World Health Organization, and several government agencies and education groups. He is the author of several chapters on education policy. His doctorate from the George Washington University focused on counseling, reading, and public policy.

G. Reid Lyon, Ph.D., has more than thirty years of experience as a public school educator, professor, research scientist, psychologist, and policymaker. Prior to his most recent positions as associate dean of the Annette Caldwell Simmons School of Education and Human Development at Southern Methodist University and distinguished professor at the School of Brain and Behavior Sciences at the University of Texas-Dallas, Dr. Lyon was chief of the Child Development and Behavior Branch within the National Institute of Child Health and Human Development (NICHD) at the National Institutes of Health (NIH) from 1992 until 2005. In 2006 Dr. Lyon was named one of the ten most influential people in American education during the last decade by the Editorial Projects in Education Research Center (*Education Week*) for his work in ensuring that scientific research occupies a central role in educational practices and policy. He was recently appointed as a Distinguished Professor of Education Leadership and Policy at Southern Methodist University in Dallas, Texas, and a Distinguished Scientist in the School of Brain and Behavior Sciences at the University of Texas, Dallas. Dr. Lyon is also the president and chief executive officer of Synergistic Education Solutions.

Elenn Steinberg is the president of the International Dyslexia Association's Rocky Mountain branch based in Glendale, Colorado. She was instrumental in working with the Colorado State Board of Education to enact state laws to support students with dyslexia. Ms. Steinberg is a national proponent for universal screening and assessment for all children in early elementary school and served as the 2009 co-chair of the Colorado Special Education Advisory Committee. She was actively involved in Colorado's Response to Intervention framework for literacy attainment and chairs "Reading in the Rockies," an annual literacy conference that provides the most comprehensive range of evidence-based information, education, and services that address literacy failure. She is a parent to a high-school-aged child with dyslexia.

This book is dedicated to the people, families, and community organizations that are trying to make the world a better place by giving all children the gift of reading literacy, education and life opportunity.

****

All proceeds and royalties from the sale of this book are donated to the International Dyslexia Association.

Made in the USA
Charleston, SC
05 November 2011